TWO DISTINCT
GOSPEL MESSAGES
OF THE
NEW TESTAMENT

GRACEWORD PUBLISHING

TWO DISTINCT GOSPEL MESSAGES OF THE NEW TESTAMENT

USING THE LITERARY STRUCTURE
OF THE NEW TESTAMENT

Dr. David Alan Greene

GraceWord Publishing, LLC
www.gracewordpublishing.com
U.S.A.

GRACEWORD PUBLISHING

To my mother Frances Mae Greene

Study to shew thyself approved unto God,
A workman that needeth not to be ashamed,
Rightly dividing the word of truth.

2 Timothy 2:15

Contents

Acknowledgements

I would like to thank the late Rev. Henry J. Harding. It was in his home Bible study that I was first introduced me to C.I. Scofield's booklet entitled Rightly Dividing the Word of Truth. In my seminary studies I was exposed to multiple systems of theology and interpretation.

I would also like to thank the late Dr. Nathan R. Killian, former president and founder of Evangelical Theological Seminary. It was his patience, guidance in my studies and personal encouragement that inspired me to complete my degrees.

Finally, my gratitude to my parents, family, and friends who listened and asked questions as I explained by journey of understanding Scripture.

Preface

This is a reprint of the dissertation for consideration towards the Doctor of Philosophy in Biblical Studies from the Evangelical Theological Seminary. The original title was "Using The Dispensational System of Theology Reveals A New Testament Chiasmus With Two Distinct Gospel Messages: One For Israel And One For The Body Of Christ." There was some discussion concerning the length of its title.

During my studies for my Bachelor of Theology, I decided that a dispensational approach to Scriptures was most logical. In spite of my protestations against studying alternative systems, I was instructed that learning these alternatives, their strengths and weaknesses, would be of value later. I can say now that the time invested in reviewing and studying these alternatives was very valuable in my understanding of and interacting with others who hold a different system as their approach.

I was affected greatly by reading Dr. Donald Grey Barnhouse's four volume Commentary on Romans. He made very clear important facts in a logical argument concerning the sinfulness of all humankind, the finished work of the Cross, and the unmerited offer of salvation to all. He also made it clear that our salvation was made perfect by the shed blood of Christ concerning our past, present, and our future sins. As the hymnist says, "Calvary covered it all."

A logical crisis occurred in my theological beliefs mid-way through my Master of Biblical Studies. While attending my daughter's baptism at a conservative Baptist church, the preacher's sermon included an admonition. He explained that we are saved by grace through faith without works. However, once we are saved, we are obligated to live up to God's standards in order for us to keep our salvation. I sat there in the congregation thinking something is wrong here. I believe that throughout my education that the Holy Spirit guided me towards understanding the Scriptures. So, here I prayed for illumination.

It was not long after that I had the pleasure of walking with one of my mentors, J. R. Lawrence. As we walked, he asked me what my reaction would be if he told me there are two distinct gospels in the

New Testament. My immediate reaction was one of shock. There was only one Cross and only one Savior. He agreed. Rather than pursuing the discussion, he asked me if I would be willing to pray about it and ask the Holy Spirit, if this was true, to show me. It was somewhat surprising to me since I had not mentioned my personal crisis to him and yet here was an opportunity to do more biblical research.

I hope that, if you are like me, you hold the Bible as the highest truth and anything that affronts it is anathema. However, we must be open to the leading of the Holy Spirit especially in the understanding of His revelation to us. This is the crisis that has evolved into more than three years of study concerning this issue. Again, I should point out that we all have our preconceived theology and, unless we are willing to be open to the moving of the Holy Spirit, we will be like the Pharisees who when hearing Christ speak deemed Him blasphemous even to the point of having Him killed.

Many people, with whom I have discussed this concept as I continued to investigate this matter, actually became very angry. One became violent; storming out of a Bible study, cursing the others and slamming the door. Another acquaintance with his Master in Divinity became so offended he started quoting Calvin and Luther in his biblical defense. He attacked C.I. Scofield, a noted dispensationalist, saying he claimed to have a doctorate when there was no record of his attaining that degree. Scofield was later president of Dallas Theological Seminary and wrote a multi-volume commentary which will be quoted later in my argument. Finally, a dear Christian friend was attending my Bible Study for seniors. She found my dispensational presentation very interesting to the point she said that the Bible suddenly made a lot more sense. However, when going to Florida for the winter, she was told by her pastor that he has never heard of such a concept and it would be best for her to stay away from me. Not one of these people argued against it using the Bible. They loved their own theology. They had learned from someone else who had another system in place. It could not be challenged without causing a crisis. However, crisis leads to resolution and the process is how we reach truth.

One could say that I am swimming against the current. It has been my observation that truth is never the popular belief. Counting the number of adherents to any particular belief is not the way to confirm proper interpretation. J.R. Lawrence reminded me of two points: (1) of the estimated billions of people on the earth prior to the Flood, only eight survived; (2) of the millions of Abraham's descendants that came out of Egypt, only two of the original men reached the shores of the Promised Land: Joshua and Caleb. There are few that will accept the truth and, although this is not an argument in favor of accepting my hypothesis, it is an indication that we should all be more like the Bereans. We read about them concerning their willingness to listen to Paul and his gospel. Speaking of the Berean Jews we read, "These were more noble than those in Thessalonica, in that they received the word with all readiness of mind, and searched the scriptures daily, whether those things were so" (Acts 17:11).

It would be both my hope and prayer that you consider the presentation carefully without prejudice. Furthermore, I urge that you would ask the Holy Spirit to lead you. If it is not of God, then there must be, without question, apparent contradictions in Scripture. However, I will present a comprehensive theological system which resolves these difficulties and presents an acceptable, comprehensive, systematic theology for the New Testament.

Outline

I. Introduction
    A. Theologically everyone starts from a different place
        1. Developed over years
        2. Different sources
        3. We need to understand where others start
        4. Popularity is not a test of truth
        5. Historical development is not an indicator
    B. Our theological system in deeply ingrained
        1. It becomes the basis of all our understanding
        2. Overlooking conflicting beliefs
    C. Need for a test to determine truth of a system
        1. Consistency throughout the entire text
        2. Comprehensiveness in applying the system to all facts
        3. Comparing system by the one that

holds together
D. The need for establishing one system of
    truth
    1. Any conflict present an indication the
        system is wrong
    2. There is no other way to achieve a
        system than trial and error
    3. The puzzle box picture is the system
        to which all the pieces must fit
    4. The system must reason from the
        general to the particular
    5. He is the Rewarder of them that dili-
        gently seek Him
E. Overcoming existing systems is like assail-
    ing a fortress

II.   Systems of theology
A. Most believers lack an established system
B. Systematic theology emphasizes the sys-
    tematization of theology
C. Consideration of different definitions and
    components of systematic theology
    1. Paul Enns
    2. Charles C. Ryrie
    3. Charles Hodge
    4. Lewis Sperry Chafer
D. Developing an acceptable system
    1. It must limit itself to biblical revela-
        tion alone

B. There are eight covenants in the Old Testament

C. Three do not pertain to Israel as they pre-date Abraham
   1. Edenic
   2. Adamic
   3. Noahic

D. Five covenants pertain exclusively to Israel
   1. Abrahamic
   2. Palestinian (Land)
   3. Mosaic
   4. Davidic
   5. New

E. Abrahamic Covenant
   1. Was non-conditional as it resulted from Abraham's faith
   2. Allegorically cannot be transferred to God's "elect" in general

F. Palestinian Covenant
   1. Ownership of the land is promised to Abraham's descendants
   2. Occupancy of the land is based upon compliance

G. Mosaic Covenant
   1. Israel accepted its terms and conditions agreeing to fulfill all its requirements
   2. Blessings and curses

3. Instituted with sacrificial system to temporarily cover non-compliance
4. Was a terrible burden for the children of Israel

H. Davidic Covenant
   1. Everlasting throne
   2. Everlasting kingdom
   3. Everlasting King to sit on David's throne

I. New Covenant
   1. Covenant was promised to the House of Israel and the House of Judah
   2. This covenant was unconditional
   3. God would fulfill this covenant Himself

VII. Prophecies exclusive to Israel

A. Prophecies and covenants are all promises when God says I will

B. Daniel is the key to understanding the fulfillment of the promises

C. Daniel's prophecy concerns the Time of the Gentiles

D. Prophecy in the past was fulfilled literally and so will the future

E. The great statue
   1. Babylonian
   2. Medo-Persian
   3. Greek

at the temple

C. This approach makes the New Testament applicable to the Church; Israel loses its distinction

D. Ryrie claims ultradispensationalism places more than one dispensation between Pentecost and the end of the church age

E. Stam claims the most important division in the Bible is between prophecy and the great mystery proclaimed by the Apostle Paul

F. Two examples cited as proof the Messiah came to Israel to fulfill prophecy

    1. I am not sent but unto the lost sheep of the house of Israel

    2. Peter told the Jews to repent and be baptized for the remission of their sins

IX. The Apostle Paul

A. What drives both the Jews and Christians to hate this man?

B. Of the twenty-eight chapters of Acts sixteen are given to the Apostle Paul

C. Paul was not the replacement for Judas

    1. He could not have met the requirements

    2. The lot fell to Matthias

D. Paul persecuted the new Jewish sect and

ment of the Time of the Gentiles
2. Then the fulfillment of the Kingdom promised to Israel will take place
K. The importance of "rightly dividing the word of truth" cannot be over-emphasized

X. The Gospels
A. The New Testament is similar to a chiasmus used in Hebrew poetry
B. The chiasmus will help us to "rightly divide" the New Testament
C. The chiasmus is symmetrically balanced and has a center focal point
1. A – The Gospels (Offer of the King and Kingdom)
2. B – Books of Acts (Transition)
3. C – Paulin Epistles (Revelation of the Mystery)
4. B' - Hebrews (Transition)
5. A' - Jewish Epistles & Revelation
D. The King and Kingdom are not allegorical but earthly
E. The Lord Jesus Christ is the rightful Heir to David's Throne
1. Matthew provides Joseph's lineage which had been cursed
2. Luke provides Mary's lineage which is legitimate
F. Israel is the sheep and the Savior is their

Shepherd
- 1. Paul never refers to the Church–the Body of Christ as sheep
- 2. I am not sent but unto the lost sheep of the house of Israel
- 3. Who are the "other sheep" John 10:14-16?

G. Scriptures in the gospels concerning the last days
- 1. The Rapture is unique to the Church–the Body of Christ
- 2. The Rapture is imminent and the Tribulation is not
- 3. The Great Commission concerns the preaching of the Gospel of the Kingdom during the last days
- 4. Commentary on "one will be taken and one will be left"

H. Tradition is the greatest obstacle to interpreting the Gospels correctly

XI. The Book of Acts

A. The book of Acts is a pivotal book in the New Testament

B. Acts is traditionally misinterpreted
- 1. Many believe the Church started in Acts 2
- 2. Some believe it was to be the model Church

3. Some believe the Church started in the Gospels and was empowered in Acts
4. The Great Commission was to be carried out by the Church in Acts
C. The book of Acts is transitional from the Gospel of the Kingdom to the Gospel of Grace preached by Paul
D. Acts 2 Church
   1. Was to remain in Jerusalem until the Comforter had come
   2. Fulfilled the prophecy given by Joel (Joel 2:28-32)
   3. Peter's sermon calls for repentance and baptism for remission of sins
   4. Activities included water baptism, fellowship, breaking bread, and praying
E. The word "church" means assembly
F. Stoning of Stephen is blasphemy of the Holy Spirit by the Jews
   1. Judgment on the Jews
   2. Introduction of Saul
G. Dislike of Paul reason his inspired revelation is ignored
H. Paul' conversion
   1. First sinner to be saved by grace through faith

A. In our chiasmus Hebrews is a book of transition
B. Who wrote Hebrews?
    1. Paul is the most common answer
    2. Luke may have transcribed Paul's letter
C. To whom was it written?
    1. Many argue it was a letter from Paul to Jewish believers
    2. To may be written to post-Rapture Jews
D. Hebrews presents Christ as the High Priest after Melchizedek
E. Definite references pertaining to the Jews
    1. The Levitical priesthood
    2. The altar
    3. The offerings
    4. The Tabernacle
    5. The Holy of Holies
    6. Baptisms until the time of reformation
F. On the night He was betrayed He was the Cup Bearer of His Blood–A Priest
G. Three roles of the Messiah
    1. The Prophet during His earthly ministry
    2. The Priest for Israel currently
    3. The King when He returns victori

ously

    H. Paul wrote Hebrews to his beloved brethren for their time of testing

XIV.   The Jewish Epistles & Revelation

    A. There are now three divisions of humanity

        1. Gentiles (the Nations)

        2. Jews (God's elect)

        3. The Church–the Body of Christ (Jew and Gentile)

    B. The Body of Christ was removed at the Rapture

    C. Jewish epistles were written with twofold purpose

        1. The original recipients

        2. The future recipients during the Tribulation

    D. The Tribulation

        1. First three and one-half years

        2. The abomination that causes desolation

        3. The remaining three and one-half years

        4. Closing with the return of their King

    E. The Jewish epistles and Revelation complete the New Testament chiasmus

XV.   Conclusion

    A. Presupposition that the Bible needs to be understood "rightly divided"

1. All Scripture is for us
2. Not all Scripture is to us
B. Examples of popular preachers
    1. Joel Osteen
    2. Rick Warren
C. Importance of being open
    1. Listen to what is being said or taught
    2. Search the Scriptures to see whether these things are so

1

An Introduction

A group of people are about to take a journey together. It is advantageous for them to have a mutual understanding of the intended itinerary and destination in advance. This would allow, in our case, the reader to anticipate the stops to be made along the way ultimately leading us to our final destination. As the tour director, I will lay out a general overview of our journey. However, with this metaphor, there is a problem–one which will greatly affect my best efforts to present my argument. We all start from different places!

Each section of our journey will play an important part in understanding the argument presented. Therefore, since we are unable to start together from the same point, we need to at least understand the starting points of others. Each of us has a different theological viewpoint which we have established over our lifetime. As such, we will consider three predominant theological positions within the evangelical community of believers. Although others exist, our examination will be limited to these three theological systems that, as a group, generally hold to the inspiration of Scripture which is the common basis of belief. Two strive for understanding Scripture based upon the original intent of the author who is writing to the original recipients. The third is more of a subjective approach to understanding Scripture.

One of the common misconceptions concerning an "indication of truth" has to do with popularity. Many point to the success of the mega-churches with hundreds of thousands of adherents. Sr. Robert Anderson offers this: ". . . truth has always been in the minority. But there is no element of cohesion in error. Among the children of error there is no bond of unity save such as depends on common hostility to truth." Some may argue that their system is true because its historical development preceded others. As an example, Covenant Theology preceded Dispensational Theology as an established theological system by about three hundred years according to ecclesiastical history. Ultimately, it should be the Bible that will be the proof of any system. Renald Showers did an excellent job when comparing two of these systems. He writes:

It should be noted . . . that correctness of a view is not proven conclusively by the fact that it was the original view. Initial impressions and conclusions of human beings in any realm of knowledge can be incorrect. Because this is true, the ultimate test of correctness for any view in the realm of theology is not the question of it being the original view, but the question of its agreement with the scriptures . . . it must agree with the teaching of the Bible. (Showers 2013, 155)

We all look at the Bible from our own theological viewpoint. Everyone, including an atheist, has a theological view. Most believers have developed an amalgamation of beliefs or doctrines which they hold to be true, whether or not these beliefs are consistent with each other. Unbeknownst to them, they have accumulated doctrine over the course of their life which stem from multiple systems. They may have begun Sunday school at an early age and over the remainder of their life they will have listened to various evangelists and preachers many of whom have different systems of interpretation. As such, they collect information and, without a consistent system within which to hold their beliefs, they must ignore any portions that are conflicting. One example would be the end times. One preacher teaches the ultimate victory of the Church over the fallen world which will bring in the Kingdom. Another teaches the Church will be raptured before the tribulation and Christ will return to earth establishing His earthly Kingdom Himself. The result is most believers must either accept or ignore the facts.

Our theological or philosophical system becomes deeply ingrained and part of who we are. Depending on the depth of our commitment, this could include our perception of everything that surrounds us. Norman Geisler, a foremost Christian apologist, calls this system a "framework." He writes:

> Once an overall framework has been determined, then it follows that whatever most consistently and comprehensively fits into that system is true. If that system of truth is not only a world view but a world and *life* view, then the applicability of that truth to life also becomes a crucial aspect of that truth. (Geisler 2003, 145)

After someone establishes their system, even if that system has conflicting beliefs, he or she almost becomes a prisoner to it; confined to interpreting everything within their system of truth. Let us consider a home being built. Before the house can be finished, the foundation must be laid and the framing completed. Once the home is finished it will be very difficult to change either the foundation or the framework upon which the entire house is held together. However, if the framing was done incorrectly the safety of both the home and its occupants is in jeopardy. This is the case when interpreting Scripture without a system or one of dubious value. How then can we know which system presents us with the best probability of a safe and true interpretation?

It has been stated that this test, one that can provide us with a determination as to which is the best system, can only be used when comparing systems and would not apply to testing truth within the system itself. Concerning this, Geisler writes, " . . . the grounds for rejecting systematic consistency . . . as a test *between* world views do not apply to using it as a test for truth *within* a given system or world view." I believe that, although this may apply to world views in general, it does not apply to Scripture due to its unique nature of infallibility. Scripture shares many of the attributes of God. It is the immutable, plenary, and authoritative Word of God. Therefore, if various systems of biblical interpretation were to be graded, it must be based upon two things: (1) consistency throughout the entire text and (2) comprehensiveness in applying the system to all the facts in Scripture including both the Old and New Testaments.

Therefore, the value of applying a system to determine truth is possible when comparing two systems by how well each one holds together. Geisler summaries:

> The main arguments against it as a test for a world view are based on the fact that more than one system might be equally systematically consistent and that the facts within a system are given meaning by that system. But once the system and therefore the ultimate meaning of all facts within it are determined, then these facts should not be interpreted in ways contrary to the system. And once it is determined that no other system is true, then there is no external competing way to interpret these. Within a given system consistency of interpretation and comprehensive coverage of all facts are definitive. Error arises when the interpretation is either internally inconsistent or else not factually all-inclusive. (Geisler

2003, 145-146)

The above approach supports the need for establishing one system in which all truth and the understanding of it can be maintained. As mentioned before, once a system has been accepted, then, by nature of the framework, all theology must be ordered within that system. The proof is the ability to consistently include all the facts within that system without causing conflict. Any conflict presents an indication that the system may be wrong. Unfortunately, there is no other way to achieve such a system other than by trial and error. To look at the facts and then create the system that holds all the facts together would be difficult lacking the overview of the entire picture.

I was teaching a men's Bible study one night where I had taken a 1,000-piece picture puzzle and broken them up into a basket. I passed the basket around and told them to take ten pieces each. Instructing them to look at their individual pieces as well as those of their neighbor's, I asked them, "Can you tell me about the picture?" They guessed a red house and a red barn, but they really weren't sure. I then held up the picture on the front of the puzzle box. It was a red covered bridge. I asked, "How many of you think that you would know where your individual pieces would go if I showed you this box at the beginning?" They unanimously agree that they would. Some of them even insinuated that it was foolish of me to expect them to do it. That is when I said, "This picture on the box is like systematic theology. Without a system, you were lost." Concerning this, E. W. Bullinger suggests:

> There is one great foundation principle in the science of LOGIC which will meet all the difficulties, if we are careful to observe it. It is this:- *We cannot reason from the paricular to the general.* That is to say, we cannot expect to find the *general* principles, which we may regard "the truth," by arguing from certain *particular parts* of the truth. On the contrary, we must reason from the *general* to the *paricular,* if we would reason accurately. (Bullinger 1993, vii)

This presents us with a conundrum. We can create our own system and test it against the components of the text to see if there is a conflict. On the other hand, we can study existing systems which have been created and modified by great students of the Bible. We are assured " . . . that He is a rewarder of them that diligently seek Him" (Heb. 11:6). An important fact is that we have human limitations as we seek to ascertain the true meaning of the text. A point Geisler clearly makes:

> It must be admitted that systematic consistency does not provide an apodictic [absolute certainty] or undeniable test for truth. No finite mind is in actual possession of *all* the facts. Nor is any finite person able to comprehend completely *all* the relationships between facts. As in almost everything else in life, probability is the guide. Whichever view *best* fits and is *most* consistent must suffice. (Geisler 2003, 146)

Again, in our testing process, we will limit our time to examining three systems that accept the Bible as God's authoritative and complete revelation to Mankind. The first rule is always: We must define our text. This requirement rules out all other sources as acceptable revelation from God. As far as extra biblical documents, they may be of interest, but not in determining Christian doctrine–truth.

While pursuing my research, I talked with numerous people, those who were willing to listen, about concepts of biblical viewpoints. To those who hold deeply their theological convictions, it is like assailing a fortress to ask them to consider an alternative. Thinking back to the time when the Lord Jesus Christ walked the earth with His disciples, the Jews held to their long-standing beliefs. They expected a powerful king to come and vanquish their enemies; not a servant. Jesus taught that He was their promised Messiah, yet they rejected Him to the point of having Him crucified. We as believers must be aware that, as humans, we tend to hold our theological "systems" and our "traditions" like possessions. The real question is whether we will put the Bible first and allow the Word of God to speak directly to us. We must be like the Bereans, "…they received the word with all readiness of mind, and searched the Scriptures daily, whether those things were so" (Acts 17:11). They eagerly listened, but then compared what was said with the Scriptures.

A test will be applied in order to determine which system is best. This test, when applied to these systems of interpretation, will be made based upon their comprehensiveness and consistency when applied to Scripture in its entirety. There is a difference between the systems and the actual interpretation and these must be in line with each other. Ryrie compares:

The difference between exegesis and the

ology is the system used. Exegesis ana-
lyzes; theology correlates those analyses.
Exegesis relates the meanings of texts;
theology interrelates those meanings.
The exegete strives to present the meaning of truth; the theologian, the system of
truth. Theology's goal, whether biblical
or systematic theology, is the systematization of the teachings under consideration. (Ryrie 1999, 18)

The system that holds the entire revelation with no
conflict would be the best system to apply to biblical
interpretation. The task of biblical interpretation is
called hermeneutics.

Since we intend to utilize hermeneutics as our
test of truth as we consider various systems, a definition would be appropriate. Roy B. Zuck, Professor of
Bible Exposition at Dallas Theological Seminary, offers this definition: "Hermeneutics . . . is the science
and art of interpreting the Bible. Another way to define hermeneutics is this: It is the science (principles)
and art (task) by which the meaning of the biblical
text is determined." Applying this to Bullinger's
statement recorded earlier, the system would be the
general and hermeneutics would be the *particular*. As
such, we must reason from the former to the latter.

Next, we will look at two conservative views concerning systematic theology from very different theological positions.

2

Systems of Theology

One may ask, "Why is a system necessary?" Many believers who lack an established system collect biblical facts, even to the point of memorization, and yet have no idea what the Bible is revealing as a whole. In this chapter, we will examine writings by well-known teachers at recognized seminaries. Their years of teaching students of the Bible give them the ability to explain various concepts concerning systems of biblical interpretation. Paul Enns gives an excellent definition of *systematic theology*:

> The term *theology* is derived from the Greek *theos,* meaning "God," and logos, meaning "word" or "discourse"; hence, "discourse about God." The word *systematic* comes from the Greek verb *sunistano,* which means "to stand together" or "to organize"; hence, systematic theo-

logy emphasizes the systematization of theology. (Enns 2008, 149)

Charles C. Ryrie is a well-known author of the *Ryrie Study Bible* and former professor at both Dallas Theological Seminary and Philadelphia College of the Bible. He offers a comparison between extracting the meaning of various verses of Scripture (exegesis) and organizing that information into a system:

> The difference between exegesis and theology is the system used. Exegesis analyzes; theology correlates those analyses. Exegesis relates the meanings of texts; theology interrelates those meanings. The exegete strives to present the meaning of truth; the theologian, the system of truth. Theology's goal, whether biblical or systematic theology, is the systematization of the teachings under consideration. (Ryrie 1999, 18)

The first theologian we will consider is Charles Hodge. He was a Presbyterian theologian and president of Princeton Theological Seminary from 1851 to 1878. He is known for being a proponent of the Covenantal systems during the 19th century. He qualifies as a representative of the evangelical position because of his belief in the authority of the Bible as the Word of God. It was his ideas that helped forge many of the beliefs currently held by evangelicals of the Reformed tradition. He begins by explaining that the Bible itself is not a system:

> The Bible is no more a system of theology than nature is a system of chemistry or of mechanics. We find in nature the facts which the chemist or the mechanical philosopher has to examine . . . to ascertain the laws by which they are determined. So the Bible contains the truths which the theologian has to collect, authenticate, arrange, and exhibit in their internal relation to each other. This constitutes the difference between Biblical and systematic theology. The office of the former is to ascertain and state the facts of Scripture. The office of the latter is to take the facts and determine their relation to each other and to cognate truths, as well as to vindicate them and show their harmony and consistency. This is not an easy task or one of slight importance. (Hodge 1997, 24)

So, a system becomes the method by which we

shape the information presented to us in Scripture.

Hodge has much to say about the necessity of creating a system in which we can organize our thoughts. He writes:

> It may be naturally asked, "Why not take the truths as God has seen fit to reveal them, and thus save ourselves the trouble of showing their relation and harmony?"

> The answer to this question is, in the first place, that it cannot be done. Such is the constitution of the human mind that it cannot help endeavoring to systematize and reconcile the facts which it admits to be true. In no department of knowledge have men been satisfied with the possession of a mass of undigested facts. And the students of the Bible can as little be expected to be thus satisfied . . . .

> Second, a much higher kind of knowledge is thus obtained than by the mere accumulation of isolated facts. . . . Without the knowledge of the laws of attraction and motion, astronomy would

be a confused and unintelligible collection of facts. What is true of other sciences is true of theology. We cannot know what God has revealed in His Word unless we understand, at least in some good measure, the relation in which the separate truths therein contained stand to each other. It cost the Church centuries of study and controversy to solve the problem concerning the person of Christ; that is, to adjust and bring into harmonious arrangement all the facts which the Bible teaches on that subject.

Third, we have no choice in this matter. If we would discharge our duty as teachers and defenders of the truth, we must endeavor to bring all the facts of revelation into systematic order and mutual relation. It is only thus that we can satisfactorily exhibit their truth, vindicate them from objections, or bring them to bear in their full force on the minds of men.

Fourth, such is the evident will of God. He does not teach men astronomy or chemistry, but He gives them the facts out of which those sciences are constructed. Neither does He teach us systematic theology, but He gives us in the Bible the truths which, properly understood and arranged, constitute the science of theology. As the facts of nature are all related and determined by physical laws, so the facts of the Bible are all related and determined by the nature of God and of His creatures. And as He wills that men should study His works and discover their wonderful organic relation and harmonious combination, so it is His will that we study His Word and learn that, like the stars, its truths are not isolated points, but systems, cycles, and epicycles in unending harmony and grandeur. Besides all this, although the Scriptures do not contain a system of theology as a whole, the Epistles of the New Testament do provide portions of that system. These are our authority and guide. (Hodge 1997, 24-25)

So, a system is a human tool devised to integrate a tremendous amount of information into a logically organized framework upon which biblical data can be attached.

Lewis Sperry Chafer was one of the founders of Dallas Theological Seminary and a proponent of the Dispensational system of biblical interpretation. In addition to being the seminary president he taught Systematic Theology for decades. Concerning this subject, he defines it thus:

> A science which follows a humanly devised scheme or order of doctrinal development and which purports to incorporate into its system all the truth about God and His universe from any and every source. Systematic Theology may be distinguished from *Natural Theology* in that Natural Theology draws its material only from nature; from *Biblical Theology* in that Biblical Theology draws its material only from the Bible; and from *Theology Proper* in that Theology Proper is restricted to the consideration of the Person of God, excluding His works.
>
> In defining Systematic or Thetic Theology, certain misleading and unwarranted terms have been employed. It has been declared to be "the science of religion"; but the term *religion* is in no sense a synonym of the Person of God and all

His works. Likewise, it has been declared to be "the scientific treatment of those truths which are found in the Bible"; but this science, while drawing the major portion of its material from the Scriptures, does, nevertheless, draw its material from any and every source. Again, Systematic Theology has been defined as the orderly arrangement of Christian doctrine; but as Christianity represents only a mere fraction of the whole field of truth relative to the Person of God and His universe, this definition is inadequate. (Chafer 1976, 1:5-6)

Chafer makes an important point: systematic theology is not about religion. It is about God's revelation of Himself, His works, and His plan for the redemption His Creation.

Having considered two theologians who hold differing views on their systems of interpretation, we need to work on achieving one that is acceptable. Concerning these two prevalent views, Paul Enns, professor at several seminaries, comments on their positions in his theological handbook:

Chafer provides a suitable definition of

systematic theology: "Systematic Theology may be defined as the collecting, scientifically arranging, comparing, exhibiting, and defending of all facts from any and every source concerning God and His works."

In an alternate definition, Charles Hodge defines theology as "the science of the facts of divine revelation so far as those facts concern the nature of God and our relation to Him, as His creatures, as sinners, and as the subjects of redemption. All these facts, as just remarked, are in the Bible."

It is apparent in these two contrasting definitions of systematic theology that Chafer holds to a wider view, emphasizing that systematic theology assimilates information about God from "any and every source"–including information outside of the Bible. Hodge restricts his definition about systematic theology to information gained from the Bible alone. (Enns 2008, 149)

There are limitations, as mentioned in the pre

vious chapter, which are the result of lack of information. We must remember that the Bible is God's revelation to Mankind. He is sovereign and chooses what He will reveal; not what we think we would like to know. Ryrie offers the following warning to students of the Word:

> In a word, the limitations of a theological system must coincide with the limitations of biblical revelation. In an effort to present a complete system, theologians are often tempted to fill in the gaps in the biblical evidence with logic or implications that may not be warranted.

> Logic and implications do have their appropriate place. God's revelation is orderly and rational, so logic has a proper place in the scientific investigation of that revelation. When words are put together in sentences, those sentences take on implications that the theologian must try to understand.

> However, when logic is used to create truth, as it were, then the theologian will be guilty of pushing his system beyond the limitations of biblical truth. Some-

times this is motivated by the desire to answer questions that the Scripture does not answer. In such cases (and there are a number of crucial ones in the Bible) the best answer is silence . . . (Ryrie 1999, 18)

It is important that we end with that limitation made clear. There is one system that, for lack of information to support their entire scheme of theology, finds it necessary to manufacture doctrine through rationalization rather than from the expressed Word of God.

In the next three chapters we will exam three predominant systems of theology. They are: Existential Theology, Covenant Theology, and Dispensational Theology.

3

The Existential System

Remembering back to the beginning, the requirement we established in order to be considered as an evangelical system of theology was the acknowledgement of Scripture as the absolute truth. I mentioned, at that point, that two strive for understanding Scripture based upon the original intent of the author. However, the other, which we are now examining, as you will see, would not meet this requirement fully. Due to its growing popularity and prevalence as a system in contemporary churches which purport to be Bible-preaching, I have decided to include them for your consideration.

Enns defines Existentialism as, "A neoorthodox expression emphasizing the spiritual encounter of man with God; it stresses the personal experience or commitment in contrast to simply believing facts or creeds." The difference between this system and the other two to follow is based upon their position on authority of Scripture. It is that position which causes this system to be viewed as liberalism by conservatives. Furthermore, if interpretation, as we will see momentarily, is based upon subjectivism and each person is entitled to interpret Scripture individually, can it truly be called a system at all? Ryrie writes, "Subjectivism stands as the hallmark of liberalism, though the focus of that subjectivism may vary with different people . . . That communication comes through human reason, feelings, or conscience. An important question would be, "What does it mean if Scripture is left to interpretation by our individual thoughts, emotions or conscience?"

Reason is in the forefront of Existentialism. It elevates Mankind's intelligence over the Word of God. No longer is there a message communicated to Mankind in God's special revelation. This makes reason the judge of truth and leaves no other authority by which the interpretation can be tested. When feelings became another method to interpret Scripture, emotions were added to rationalism causing religious experiences, personal feelings, and personal awareness to enter into the understanding of Scripture. Conscience became the authority and the test of interpretation. However, Paul writes: "None is righteous, no, not one; no one understands; no one seeks for God. All have turned aside; together they have become worthless; no one does good, not even one" (Rom. 10b-12). This is God's position on the ability of Mankind to seek His truth independently.

Although Existentialism is not classified as Liberalism, it shares some common beliefs. Ryrie explains:

> Neo-orthodoxy has sometimes been classed with liberalism and sometimes with conservatism. The reason for this confusion is that, on the one hand, it broke with liberalism by insisting that God, not man, must initiate revelation (and thus seemed to be conservative); while, on the other hand, it continued to teach liberal views concerning the Bible (and thus seemed to be liberal) . . .
>
> Though neoorthodoxy seeks objectivity in God's sovereign initiative, it practices subjectivism in the experiences of faith's encounters. Even though the Bible is involved in those experiences, it is not allowed to be the ultimate judge of those experiences. Neo-orthodoxy lacks an external, objective standard of authority.

(Ryrie 1999, 21)

With the existential system, Scripture is interpreted based upon one's own reasoning, feelings, and conscience. So, how well does that work?

I will share a personal experience. In the same men's Bible study that I mentioned before, we were studying 1 Corinthians 15, a critical part of Paul's gospel message. These men had faithfully attended this study for at least three years with me teaching Scripture using the dispensational system. That night we had an unexpected visit from our interim pastor. When I got finished explaining the text, everyone thought about it and then turned to the pastor for his reaction. He thought for a moment and remarked that it was a very interesting interpretation of Scripture; one that he had never heard before. Then he said, "But, we really can't know what the Bible says." Everyone in the study was shocked. What could he mean? I respect him as a person too much to argue with him in front of a class. However, the following week I brought in *The Moody Handbook of Theology* and read the definition of "existentialism" without mentioning the word–the same definition in the beginning of this chapter. The men recognized the position of the pastor from the previous week. I used it to explain that changing your system of theology will change your interpretation.

This information was presented because there are many people who claim they are Christian because they attend a Bible-preaching church. Millions of people are in delusion. The Bible has a message from God to Mankind. Consider a church whose pastor has no idea what the message of the Bible is. Now consider the following passage written by Paul, stop for a moment, and then think about it. "For whosoever shall call upon the name of the Lord shall be saved. How then shall they call on him in whom they have not believed? And how shall they believe in him of whom they have not heard? And how shall they hear without a preacher?" (Rom. 10:13-14). As a test of interpretation, I believe that existentialism, as a method, fails miserably and we will move on to the next two systems for consideration.

4

The Covenant System

This system, in my opinion, is worth understanding. Its commitment to biblical authority is never questioned. Before we start our analysis, it would be beneficial to provide some historical information about this theological "camp" and the other names by which it is known. This system may be referred to as Calvinism, the Reformed Tradition, or Replacement Theology, or Covenant Theology. An explanation of these individual names will follow later. However, Enns offers an excellent introductory definition:

> Covenant Theology is a system of interpreting the Scriptures on the basis of two covenants: the covenant of works and the covenant of grace. Some covenant theologians specify three covenants: works, redemption, and grace. Covenant theol-

ogy teaches that God initially made a covenant of works with Adam, promising eternal life for obedience and death for disobedience. Adam failed, and death entered the human race. God, however, moved to resolve man's dilemma by entering into a covenant of grace through which the problem of sin and death would be overcome. Christ is the ultimate mediator of God's covenant of grace. (Enns 2008, 531)

Here we need to incorporate the meaning of a new term, *covenant*, into our discussion. Most people are familiar with marriage being a covenant because it involves three parties: the husband, the wife, and God. In theological terms, it has a more significant meaning.

The word covenant as used in the Old Testament was derived ". . . from a verb signifying to cut or divide, an allusion to the sacrificial custom in connection with covenant-making . . . it does not in itself contain the idea of joint obligation, it mostly signifies an obligation undertaken by a single person." This would mean that one of the parties of the covenant failing to uphold their obligation under the agreement would not negate the obligation of the other parties to complete the obligation. Therefore, when God enters into a covenant relationship, regardless of the other parties' ability to fulfill their obligations, He will fulfill the agreement.

Historically, the original intent of the Scriptures was forsaken for the traditions of men. It had become a dark time for the Church and God brought about a change. Enns describes it:

> The Reformation marked a major turning point in the doctrinal development of the church. For the preceding one thousand years the authority of the church had developed continuously until the tradition of the Roman Catholic Church and the authority of the papacy determined what the people were to believe. The Reformation changed all that. (Enns 2008, 471)

The leaders of the Reformation affirmed the Bible and not the church as the final authority. It was this belief of *Sola Scriptura*, meaning "only Scripture", which cause believers to focus their attention on understanding the meaning of the Bible and developing a system of theology as a framework to hold those meanings.

Returning to Scripture as an authority was soon overcome with another problem. Over time Greek philosophy had entered Christianity through Christian biblical scholars in Alexandria in Egypt. They developed a method of interpretation called the *Alexandrian School*. Their approach had become, by nature, *allegorical*. Zuck provides this explanation:

> Allegorizing is searching for a hidden or a secret meaning underlying but remote from and unrelated in reality to the more obvious meaning of the text. In other words, the literal reading is a sort of code, which needs to be deciphered to determine the more significant and hidden meaning. In this approach the literal is superficial; the allegorical is the true meaning. (Zuck 1991, 29)

It is this allegorical method of interpretation that led to their interpretation of the word *ekklesia* which is translated as "church." This word would mean a people "called out" of a larger group, a group set aside or brought together. In mathematics, it would be a subset of a larger set. However, this word (translated as "assembly" in Acts 19:32) is used to denote a riotous group of merchants angry at Paul for his infringement upon their lucrative trade surrounding the idol Diana.

The Covenant Theologians allegorize "the church" to mean the "elect", a single group of people called out of the unwashed masses by God as his chosen people. This leads them to rationalize: if Israel is God's "elect" in the Old Testament and the Church is God's "elect" in the New Testament, then they must be the same. Therefore, their interpretation has the Church replacing Israel as His chosen people and, thereby, earning their system the name "replacement theology." Enns agrees:

> This is new terminology for covenant theology, which teaches that the church has replaced Israel in God's program. It views the covenantal promises to Israel as conditional, with Israel failing to meet the conditions. The promised blessings to Israel have been relegated to the church. (Enns 2008, 537)

We read above the definition of "covenant" meant that if one party failed to meet their obligations, the other Party, that being God, would rise to meet the other party's obligation. Such was the case at the Cross. Our Lord and Savior met our obligation to God on our behalf. The Reformed theological position outlined by the acronym T-U-L-I-P, which we will expound on shortly, admits this very fact. God did for us what we could not do for ourselves. Would this not include Israel and their covenant-breaking actions as well?

T.U.L.I.P

This has to do with the question of God's sovereignty and man's participation in the act of regeneration. In the acronym, the "T" stands for *total depravity* of man in that man is unable, because of his sinful state, to have any part in searching after God. God must initiate or provide the necessary action. To the unsaved, the gospel is foolishness and their eyes are blinded by the god of this world (cf. 1 Cor. 1:18; 2 Cor. 4:4). The "U" represents God's *unconditional election* of who will be saved and who will not. The Reformed position is that man plays no part at all in the salvation process because of his helpless state. Hodge summarized three positions as he sees it:

> Pelagians [free will advocated] deny the necessity of any supernatural influence of the Spirit in the regeneration and sanctification of men. Semi-Pelagians admit the necessity of such divine influence to assist the enfeebled powers of man in the

work of turning unto God, but claim that the sinner cooperates in that work and that upon his voluntary cooperation the issue depends. Augustine and Protestants [those who hold to the Reformed tradition] ascribe the whole work of regeneration to the Spirit of God, the soul being passive therein, the subject and not the agent of change . . . (Hodge 1997, 308)

Hodge is proposing that man has no part in salvation not even the act of accepting an offer of free salvation. Is accepting something for free considered a work? In my readings it was interesting to find how the majority of Reformed collectively refer to their founders as "the divines" as if to imply that their writings are inspired and, therefore, authoritative. If this was true, then it would be in direct conflict with Scripture (*cf.* Rev. 22:18-19).

Concerning the concept of *unconditional election,* the Reformed cite the example of the potter and the clay in Jeremiah. They assert God alone is sovereign and, like the potter, will decide the purpose for each of His creatures. When we examine the Scripture, we need to answer the question, "To whom is He speaking?" We turn to the text for our answer: "'Can I not, O house of Israel, deal with you as this potter *does?'* declares the LORD. 'Behold, like the clay in the potter's hand, so are you in My hand, O house of Israel'" (Jer. 18:6). This would be a blatant misapplication of Scripture to apply this verse to the Church unless, of course, you believe, as they do, that Israel and the Church are one in the same.

I agree with man's total depravity. In our fallen state we are all helpless. God offers the gift of salvation. He enables to us to accept His gracious offer, but many, unfortunately, choose to reject Him. Those who accept His gracious offer, He also foreknew. Man's free will is certainly within the circumference of God's sovereignty and in no way limits God's divine plans.

The "L" is for *limited atonement.* Duane Edward Spencer is typical in his wording when he writes:

> We now come to what may well be the most difficult of the *Five Points of Calvinism* because the Christian community has been so emotionally conditioned by false practices rising out of false doctrine related to raising up missionaries and collecting funds for same.

When we speak of the meritorious work of Christ on the cross, do we rightfully say that He died for all men equally and alike (as say the Arminians), or do we more accurately state (with the Calvinists) that Christ died for the elect only? (Spencer 1979, 45)

So far, we have an unconditional choosing by God as to who will be saved and who will not. To this we add that the efficacious work of the cross does not apply to all, but to only a few–only to those whom God has elected in advance.

Robert P. Lightner, professor of Systematic Theology at Dallas Theological Seminary, is a professed four-point Calvinist. He puts this matter into a more proper perspective, "Though personal faith in Christ the Savior is necessary, faith does not produce the new life. Human faith and divine regeneration occur at the same time, but one is man's responsibility as he is enabled by the Holy Spirit and the other is the work of God imparting the divine life." He openly refutes the Calvinist's position when he writes, ". . . The Bible does not teach that God's electing choice is redemptive or that Christ died only for the elect. Neither does it teach that one believes or receives Christ as Savior because He has been regenerated. It is always the other way around in the Bible. Personal faith in Christ as Savior results in salvation. It is not the result of it."

Dave Hunt points out that *limited atonement* is a key point in the Calvinists' argument, yet it is controversial even within their camp. Concerning this Hunt writes:

> Limited Atonement is one point that even Calvinists find difficult to accept. Certainly Spurgeon, at times, contradicted that which at other times he affirmed . . .

> The Calvinist recognizes that Unconditional Election and Limited Atonement "must stand or fall together. We cannot logically accept one and reject the other." But the Bible repeatedly declares that Christ died for all mankind that the gospel is offered and equally available to all, and that God wants all to be saved. Definitions of words must be changed to deny this clear biblical teaching.

> Even John MacArthur acknowledges that God *desires* all men to be saved–but

then he says that God inexplicably doesn't elect and predestine to salvation multitudes of those He desires to be saved. Odd, indeed, considering the emphasis Calvinists put on sovereignty, that God doesn't sovereignly fulfill His own desire! (Hunt 2006, 298-299)

In fact, Lightner writes, "I find deep and perplexing difficulties with the limited view of the atonement. Limited atonement is quite consistent with the other points of Calvinism, but is irreconcilable with the whole of Scripture." When discussing these points with my Calvinist friend he refers to these seemingly obvious contradictions as "tensions" and states that he is willing to accept these apparent contradictions upon faith and await the final explanation in glory. These "tensions" actually mark the failure of the test we defined previously.

The next letter in the acronym is "I" which stands for *irresistible grace*. Spencer writes, "The Calvinist insists that salvation is based on the free will of God, and since God is omnipotent, His grace cannot be resisted." Hodge explains there are two types of grace: one is common, or general, and the other efficacious. He writes:

Common grace, or that influence of the Spirit which is granted more or less to all men, is often effectually resisted . . . But since the special work of regeneration is the effect of almighty power, it can no more be resisted than the act of creation. The effect follows immediately on the will of God, as when He said, "Let there be light," and light was. (Hodge 1992, 429)

It certainly sounds like the common grace extended to all men can be rejected by them based upon their free will. We also read: "The general work of the Spirit upon the unregenerate, or common grace, simply refers to God's undeserved favor displayed toward all." Hunt makes it clear:

Irresistible Grace is essential in the Calvinist theory of salvation. No one can resist God's savings grace, irresistibly imposed upon those whom He has predestined to eternal life . . .

Sadly, this doctrine, too–like all of TULIP–leads to a denial of God's love, mercy, and grace as revealed in Scripture.

Allegedly, God has created all men incapable of choosing to seek Him and of believing the gospel. The only hope is in God himself sovereignly regenerating the sinner–but He only does this for a limited elect and damns the rest in order to prove His sovereignty and justice. Such is the message of TULJP. (Hunt 1992, 362-363)

There is no choice for those predestined to eternal damnation without a universal offer of salvation!

The final letter is "P" for *perseverance of the saints*. Eternal security means "once saved; always saved" or, in other words, the assurance of salvation for the believer. Spencer summarizes this for us:

The Calvinists taught that the saints, otherwise known as the "elect," can never be lost once their salvation is by the will of the unchanging, omnipotent God. Since no *condition* in man determines his being chosen, because Scripture teaches *unconditional election,* it stands to reason that there is nothing he can do to get himself "unsaved" once he has been saved by God's grace. (Spencer 1979, 63)

Lightner asks the question, "How can believers gain assurance?" He answers, "Genuine assurance of the forgiveness of sins can be gained through three basic means: the Word of God, the witness of the Spirit of God, and the walk of the child of God." Although this sounds like the inclusion of works in addition to grace, Lightner offers subsequent remarks, somewhat untypical of a Calvinist, to clarify his position:

> Fact, faith, and feeling are all important for the child of God. The relation of these to each other and to the matter of assurance is vital. The facts of God's Word are the most important. What He has said about man's sin, Christ's work, and man's need is all determinative. Believing and then acting upon these facts, man receives Christ as Savior. The resultant emotional feelings will vary with each individual.

> Our assurance must rest in the facts and our acceptance of the Savior of whom they speak. Our confidence should never rest in passing and changing emotions we experience.

Be confident of your security in Christ. It does not depend on you, your efforts, or your feelings. It depends only on Christ, "the author and finisher of our faith" (Heb.12:2). (Lightner 1991, 247)

It must be carefully observed that *perseverance of the saints* does not refer to works in the sense that Paul wrote to the Ephesians, "For it is by grace you have been saved, through faith–and this is not from yourselves, it is the gift of God– not by works, so that no one can boast" (Eph. 2:8-9). I have found the majority of churches do not preach "grace plus nothing." Most have added a requirement whereby salvation is achieved by "grace plus works." R. C. Sproul writes on the Ligonier Ministries' website concerning this, "So the old axiom in Reformed theology about the perseverance of the saints is this: If you have it–that is, if you have genuine faith and are in a state of saving grace–you will never lose it. If you lose it, you never had it."

Next, we will begin our examination of the last of the three systems. However, since the role of Israel is critical to the interpretation of Scripture, we must divide our consideration of Dispensational Theology into two parts: Creation to Moses and Moses to Eternity. Between these two parts, almost like a parenthetical interruption, we will temporarily divert our attention to examining the covenants and prophecies of the Old Testament.

If we choose to believe these covenants and promises apply exclusively to Israel, then we will see them play an important role in God's future plan of redemption. Understanding Israel's role will be critical.

5

The Dispensational System
Part 1

Creation To Moses

The system of Dispensational Theology is not unlike its counterpart in Covenant Theology. However, whereas the latter establishes its structure based upon covenants in the Bible, the former uses the stewardships or administrations in which God manages His Creation. As a definition, Showers writes, "Dispensational Theology can be defined very simply as a system of theology which attempts to develop the Bible's philosophy of history on the basis of the sovereign rule of God. It represents the whole of Scripture and history as being covered by several dispensations of God's rule." The origin of the word *dispensation* comes from the Greek word *oijkonomiva* in the New Testament which is translated as "the management of a household; a stewardship." Showers adds, ". . . the term *dispensation* . . . could be defined as *a particular way of God's administering His rule over the world as He progressively works out His purpose for world history.*"

There are three key critical factors which make the Dispensational system different. The first is the recognition that Israel and the Church–the Body of Christ are two separate and distinct entities in God's plan. This is contrary to the Covenant system which believes that Israel is the group of true believers and, therefore, the Church existed in the Old Testament. The second is the commitment to the literal-historical-grammatical method of hermeneutics. Ryrie writes, ". . . dispensationalism claims to employ principles of literal, plain, normal, or historical-grammatical interpretation consistently." Comparatively, the Covenant system uses two methods of hermeneutics: the historical-grammatical approach for most of Scripture in addition to using the allegorical method on prophetic text specifically in regard to Israel and the future Kingdom. The allegorical approach allows them to spiritualize the text to mean something other than its plain meaning. Finally, there is the difference in the ultimate purpose of God's plan. The Covenant theologian would say the Bible is the record of God's redemption of Mankind. Although that is important, it does not take into consideration all of God's plans. Ryrie and Showers agree on these factors. Concerning the ultimate purpose, Showers submits:

> Thus, the ultimate purpose of history has to be large enough to incorporate all of God's programs, not just one of them. Dispensational Theology proposes that the glory of God through the demonstration that He alone is the sovereign God is the only purpose capable of doing this. It also is convinced that the Scriptures indicate that this is the ultimate purpose of history. (Showers 2013, 53)

Before moving on, it is important to point out that there are three distinct groups of people upon this world–Gentile, Jew, and the Church–the Body of Christ. Matthew McGee provides us with an excellent resource to help distinguish these groups. (See Appendix, Fig. 1.) Once we understand their unique role in God's plan, we can apply that understanding to our interpretation of Scripture from a Dispensational point of view. There are different viewpoints concerning the number of dispensations, however, the most prevalent is the number seven. We will examine these briefly for a basic understanding. It is best done by the use of the chart provided and taking the time to read the Bible and see the change of administrations.

First, there is the Dispensation of Innocence, Adamic Age, beginning with Adam and Eve's creation and ending with their failure. As the federal head of Mankind, Adam's sin inherently brought upon all of us the curse of God as our punishment. Expelled from Paradise, the couple are instructed to sin not and fill the earth. Left to their own consciences, Adam and Eve started their family during what is termed the Dispensation of Conscience or the Antediluvian Age which means the age before the Flood.

The earth was filled with sin and no one knew God. Christ makes a comparison of this age to the people in the last days (*cf.* Mat. 24:37-39). Mankind failed again and the earth was flooded destroying all except eight people, the family of Noah as he listened to God. This began the third dispensation, Human Government, with instructions to go and fill the earth. Capital punishment was instituted at this time. Noah's sons were told by God, "...Be fruitful, and multiply, and replenish the earth" (Gen 9:1). However, instead of covering the earth as instructed by God, they built the first city, Babel. There they began to worship other gods by building a tower unto the heavens. God judged them, but instead of destroying them, he scattered them throughout His creation. This was the beginning of the Nations which the Hebrews call *goyim* and later became synonymous with the word *Gentiles*. This records God's third attempt and Mankind's subsequent failure. It will be shown in a chart, referred to above, that this segment of Mankind still exists and will play a major part in the finale recorded for us in Revelation.

God decided to carve out a portion of Mankind just for Himself. For this He chose a man named Abram from whom He could build a separate nation of people for Himself. What would cause God to choose this single individual? The answer is, "And [Abram] believed in the LORD; and He counted it to [Abram] for righteousness" (Gen. 15:6). He believed God at his Word. What was it that he believed? "By faith Abraham, when he was called to go out into a place which he should after receive for an inheritance, obeyed; and he went out, not knowing whither he went" (Heb. 11:8). Abraham was the beginning of the Dispensation of Promise or the Abrahamic Age. The remainder of the Old Testament records the history of Abraham and his descendants. Abraham had a grandson named Jacob. God changed Jacob's name to Israel and he had twelve sons–one for each of the Twelve Tribes. A great famine drove the descendants of Abraham down into Egypt.

There Abraham's children grew great in number during the time they stayed there and became under great oppression. On the night of their deliverance, recorded as the Passover, God saved them and led them all out into the desert. We read, "Now the sojourning of the children of Israel, who dwelt in Egypt, was four hundred and thirty years. And it came to pass at the end of the four hundred and thirty years, even the selfsame day it came to pass, that all the hosts of the LORD went out from the land of Egypt" (Ex. 12:40-41). It was while they sojourning in the desert that Moses presents to them the Mosaic Covenant as the Suzerain Who vanquished Israel's foes and now promises protection under an agreement which stipulates their obligations. It was at the point of the offer and acceptance of this agreement that the Age of Promise ended and the Mosaic Age or the Dispensation of Law began.

Out of the all the *nations*, the Lord God has now created a separate, holy nation unto Himself with strict instructions enumerated in the Mosaic Law. We will examine this more fully in the section concerning the Covenants of Israel.

During the Mosaic Age or the Dispensation of Law, the fifth in our list, God implemented the sacrificial system at the same time as the Law was instituted. God, knowing full well that Mankind could never meet His requirements, provided a means by which the penalty of breaking the Law would be covered temporarily until such time as a permanent Sacrifice would be provided. The Old Testament ends in this Age of Law in expectation of the fulfillment of prophecies or a coming Redeemer. We will complete the remaining two dispensations in a future chapter. However, we must temporarily suspend our examination of the remaining dispensations to examine the Covenants and Promises as recorded in the Old Testament.

6

Covenants With Israel

The word "covenant" is most commonly used in a legal context with its Latin origin (con venire) conveying the meaning of "coming together." It contemplates two or more parties coming together to make a contract thereby agreeing on assurances, conditions, benefits, and each party having the responsibility of upholding the contract in its entirety. Historically, the covenant includes some aspect of a blood sacrifice. In the marriage covenant three parties are involved: the husband, the wife, and the Sovereign God. Jewish couples were required to provide proof of the consummation of the marriage by providing blood-stained sheets. The sacred aspect of a covenant was not taken lightly. Clarence Larkin offers his definition:

> A Covenant is an agreement or contract between men, or between men and God.

Generally, it is based on certain conditions agreed upon. Sometimes, as between God and man, it is unconditional. God's covenants with man originate with Him, and generally consist of a promise based on the fulfilment of certain conditions. God has made eight Covenants with man. They all relate to the earth. Each one introduces a New Dispensation. Six of them were given to individual and representative men, as Adam, Noah and Abraham, and went into effect during their lives except the one given to David, which took effect at the birth of Jesus. Each one has a time element and expires at a certain time. (Larkin 2011, XXVI 149)

All eight covenants are found in the Old Testament. Three will not be reviewed as they do not pertain to Israel specifically. Each of these three covenants predates the appearance of Abram. They are: the Edenic (Gen. 1:28-30; 2:15-17), the Adamic (Gen. 3:14-19), and the Noahic (Gen.8:20 – 9:17). The five covenants we will consider are those covenants which God made specifically with descendants of Abraham. These are: Abrahamic, Palestinian (Land), Mosaic, Davidic, and the New Covenant. As we review each of these we will examine whether they are conditional or non-conditional.

Abrahamic Covenant

The covenant which God made with Abraham was non-conditional and resulted from Abraham's faith in God. It is recorded for us in Genesis (12:1-3; 13:14-17, 15:1-18). Chafer briefly summaries, "This covenant guarantees everlasting blessings upon Abraham, his seed, and all the families of the earth." Enns presents it as being two components. First, Abraham would be the ". . . Father of a nation through whom God would one day administer His rule over the world . . ." and God gave him a ". . . covenant which promised: (a) land, (b) posterity, (c) blessing." Enns goes on to point out that these three promises provide a framework for the subsequent covenants namely: the Palestinian Covenant (land), the Davidic Covenant (seed), and the New Covenant (blessing). The common denominator in all five covenants is Abraham–a man of faith. (*cf*. Heb 11:8-19)

Whether from a dispensational or covenant theology, the importance of the Abrahamic Covenant cannot be over emphasized. It plays a decisive role between two opposing theological systems. Dispensationally, this marks the beginning of the Age of

Promise which is extended to a particular group of people–the Jews. The nations, also called the Gentiles, are still under the Age of Human Government. It is important to consider that the blessings which the Gentiles would receive, at this point, are through Israel who were to be a nation of priests on their behalf. The allegorical interpretation views Abraham as the representative of the people of faith who they collectively call "the elect." This rationalization allows them to transfer the promises to God's elect, regardless of the intent of the covenant, to another party consider "the elect."

Returning to the covenant under consideration, it all depends on whether the covenant is conditional or unconditional. Concerning this, Showers responds:

> If the Abrahamic Covenant is *unconditional* (not dependent upon the obedience of Abraham, Isaac, Jacob, and their physical descendants, the people of Israel, for the fulfillment of its promises), then every promise of that covenant must be fulfilled including the promises that Israel would be given *forever* the land described in Genesis 15:18 and that the

Abrahamic Covenant would be an *everlasting* covenant for Israel. This would mean that Israel will last forever as a people and that God has a future program for that nation and its land. It would also mean that the biblical prophecies concerning the future of Israel and its land are to be interpreted literally and that the Dispensational–Premillennial view of those prophecies is correct.

By contrast, if the Abrahamic Covenant is *conditional* (dependent upon the obedience of Abraham, Isaac, Jacob, and the people of Israel for the fulfillment of its promises), then not every promise of that covenant has to be fulfilled. Disobedience by Abraham, Isaac, Jacob, or the people of Israel could nullify the fulfillment of the covenant's promises. In light of such disobedience, Israel would not have to be given the land of Canaan *forever*, the Abrahamic Covenant would not have to be an *everlasting* covenant for Israel, the biblical prophecies concerning the future of Israel and its land could be interpreted allegorically or spiritualized, and the Dispensational-Premillennial view of those prophecies would be wrong. (Showers 2013, 60)

To the average Christian these may seem like splitting hairs, but this is the key to whether Israel remains the recipient of the promises made to Abraham and the four other covenants listed above connected to it. Here is the argument:

Theologians disagree concerning whether the Abrahamic Covenant is conditional or unconditional. Dispensational Theologians contend that the covenant is unconditional. Covenant Theologians disagree with each other on this issue. Many Covenant Theologians say that the Abrahamic Covenant is conditional, while others say that it is unconditional but that the national promises to Israel must be interpreted allegorically, not literally. (Showers 2013, 61)

The Scriptural references used to establish the conditional nature of the promises must be examined. "And when Abram was ninety years old and nine, the LORD appeared to Abram, and said unto him, I am the Almighty God; walk before me, and be thou perfect. And I will make my covenant between me and thee, and will multiply thee exceedingly" (Gen. 17:1-2). Reading this we need to not change the words to conform to our theology. For example, "Today, you will go to school and get an 'A' on both your tests. And I will go food shopping." This is clearly not an "if-then" statement which is required for a condition. In another similar reference we read, "And said, By myself have I sworn, saith the LORD, for because thou hast done this thing, and hast not withheld thy son, thine only son: That in blessing I will bless thee, and in multiplying I will multiply thy seed as the stars of the heaven, and as the sand which is upon the sea shore; and thy seed shall possess the gate of his enemies; And in thy seed shall all the nations of the earth be blessed; because thou hast obeycd my voice" (Gen. 22:16-18). There is no threat of loss conditioned upon Abraham's actions. Instead, it is an abundant increase of the promises already made to him in the original covenant.

Both of these verses are recorded after the original covenant had been made. Neither by man or God, a covenant, once it has been established, is unchangeable. Paul writes to the Galatians, "Brethren, I speak after the manner of men; Though it be but a man's covenant, yet if it be confirmed, no man disannulleth, or addeth thereto" (Gal. 3:15). Peter points out why we can always trust the Bible, "But the word of the Lord endureth for ever" (1 Pet. 1:25).

Palestinian (Land) Covenant

"In the same day the LORD made a covenant with Abram, saying, Unto thy seed have I given this land, from the river of Egypt unto the great river, the river Euphrates . . ." (Gen. 15:18). Israel for a time possessed their land and reached the zenith of their past under the rule of King Solomon. However, to date, they have never reached the full boundaries promised to Abraham. Never has God not fulfilled the promises he has made. This would mean that the fulfillment will be in the future. The promise made to Abraham did not become a covenant until later. "The Palestinian Covenant was established by God with Israel after the establishment of the Mosaic Covenant, and it is separate from the Mosaic Covenant." The future possession of the land was promised to Abraham. However, the occupancy of the land was conditioned upon Israel's actions as recorded in the blessings and curses. (*cf.* Deut. 28) This does not create a condition of the ultimate possession of the land by Israel, but makes it based solely upon God's providence to fulfill the obligation.

Mosaic Covenant

The Mosaic Covenant is recorded in the Book of Exodus (Ex. 20:1-31:18). Chafer observes that it comprises:

> . . . three parts, namely, the commandments, the judgments, and the ordinances which, in turn, directed the moral, social, and religious life of Israel and imposed penalties for every failure. The Mosaic Covenant is a covenant of works. Its blessings were made to depend on human faithfulness. It also provided the remedial sacrifices by which the sin and failure of those under the covenant could be cared for and they restored to right relations with God. (Chafer 1976, 1:42-43)

This marks, for the Jews only, the end or the Age of Promise and the beginning of the Age of Law. Fulfillment of the Law as outlined in the Pentateuch would be the promises to protect and preserve them as His peculiar people, but the weight of the Law was great. "And Moses came and called for the elders of the people, and laid before their faces all these words which the LORD commanded him. And all the people answered together, and said, All that the LORD hath spoken we will do. And Moses returned the words of the people unto the LORD" (Ex. 19:7-8). It was upon their acceptance of the terms and conditions that they were now under the bondage of their agreement–the Mosaic Law. As such, they would receive the blessings for compliance and the curses for failure to meet these requirements. (*cf.* Deut.28)

There are two important verses to include here. The preface to the curses reads, "But it shall come to pass, if thou wilt not hearken unto the voice of the LORD thy God, to observe to do all his commandments and his statutes which I command thee this day; that all these curses shall come upon thee, and overtake thee. . ." (Deut. 28:15). Note particularly, the adjective before the commandments. It says *all*. So, the failure to do *all* would result in their loss of blessings and result in curses. That was bondage. Towards the end of this chapter of blessings and curses, we read with almost ominous awe, "And the LORD shall scatter thee among all people, from the one end of the earth even unto the other; and there thou shalt serve other gods . . . And among these nations shalt thou find no ease, neither shall the sole of thy foot have rest: but the LORD shall give thee there a trembling heart, and failing of eyes, and sorrow of mind…" (vv. 64-65). This proud nation will eventually be brought to realize their need for total dependence on their God.

The effect of the Law was great as it permeated the Jewish culture and their pursuit of achieving acceptance by God. Later, the importance of acceptance by their peers became their primary motivation as each strove to demonstrate their own level of righteousness. This was particularly evident in the Pharisees, the representatives of Israel during the time of their Messiah. It also created an opportunity to judge each other based upon their compliance with the sacred mandates. This is an important fact to remember when comparing the Dispensation of Grace, the Church Age, with the purpose and fulfillment of the Law.

Davidic Covenant

This covenant was made with David, King of Israel, who was called a man after God's own heart and reigned as their second king. His son, Solomon, was the third king and was responsible for bringing Israel to its height of glory. Yet, neither would be

Israel's greatest King as promised in the Davidic Covenant. Chafer summaries, "The Davidic Covenant (2 Sam. 7 :5-19), which secures three paramount advantages to Israel through the Davidic House, namely, an everlasting throne, an everlasting kingdom, and an everlasting King to sit on David's throne." This is a promise made to David as an unconditional covenant which is the hope of all living Jews both in biblical times as well as the present.

The New Testament gives greater impetus to this covenant. By presenting His lineage at the opening of the Gospel of Matthew, its purpose was to establish the validity of the Lord Jesus Christ as the rightful Heir to the throne of David. We read, "The book of the generation of Jesus Christ, the son of David, the son of Abraham" (Matt. 1:1). Remember, later upon the triumphal entry into Jerusalem on Palm Sunday, the crowds greeted Him as He entered the city. "And the multitudes that went before, and that followed, cried, saying, Hosanna to the son of David: Blessed is he that cometh in the name of the Lord; Hosanna in the highest" (v. 21:9). It was not long after this entry in which the Lord Jesus Christ, the rightful King of Israel, was crucified by them. Consider the irony here. The people were all obligated under the Law and all were worthy of death, but the High Priest spoke truth, "Now Caiaphas was he, which gave counsel to the Jews, that it was expedient that *one man* should die for the people" (Jn. 18:14). Again, John writes:

> And Pilate wrote a title, and put it on the cross. And the writing was JESUS OF NAZARETH THE KING OF THE JEWS. This title then read many of the Jews: for the place where Jesus was crucified was nigh to the city: and it was written in Hebrew, and Greek, and Latin. Then said the chief priests of the Jews to Pilate, Write not, The King of the Jews; but that he said, I am King of the Jews. Pilate answered, What I have written I have written. (Jn. 19:19-22)

This covenant promise remains unfulfilled. However, we can be confident that He Who has promised is faithful. Showers writes:

> It should be noted that God stated no conditions in the content of the Davidic Covenant when He established it with David. This indicates that the Davidic Covenant is unconditional in nature. It depends totally upon

the faithfulness of God for the fulfillment of its promises. (Showers 2013,
87)

We will see in the next covenant that it will be God
that fulfills the requirements under a newer covenant in His blood which will supersede the older
one.

New Covenant

This covenant, it is believed, is the justification
of the name New Testament and, therefore, it is as-
sumed by the majority of Christendom that this covenant belongs to Christians. This, however, it is not
that case and shall be proven without doubt by using
the literal-historical-grammatical approach. The covenant is promised in Jeremiah 31:31, but similar
promises concerning this were made in Isaiah 59-20-
21, Jeremiah 50:4-5, Ezekiel 34:25-30; 37:21-28.

From the following excerpt from Jeremiah, it is
clear that this is a promise that has not yet been fulfilled:

Behold, the days come, saith the
LORD, that I will make a new covenant with the house of Israel, and

with the house of Judah: Not according to the covenant that I made with their fathers in the day that I took them by the hand to bring them out of the land of Egypt; which my covenant they brake, although I was an husband unto them, saith the LORD: But this shall be the covenant that I will make with the house of Israel;

After those days, saith the LORD, I will put my law in their inward parts, and write it in their hearts; and will be their God, and they shall be my people. And they shall teach no more every man his neighbor, and every man his brother, saying, Know the LORD: for they shall all know me, from the least of them unto the greatest of them, saith the LORD: for I will forgive their iniquity, and I will remember their sin no more. (Jer. 31:31-34)

It is important to note in the first two lines above that the new covenant is being promised to "the house of Israel" and the "house or Judah." First, without allegorizing the text, if we accept it at face value, that is as plain text, then it would have to be interpreted to mean that the Jews are the beneficiaries of this pending new covenant. Second, there is other evidence that this pertains to the Jews: "the covenant that I made with their fathers," "took them by the hands to bring them out of the land or Egypt," and "I will put *my law* in their inward parts."

As a closing remark to this covenant, Showers offers us this:

> Two things can be said concerning the nature of the New Covenant. First, God intended it to be an *unconditional* covenant. God stated no conditions in the passages which deal with the covenant. This meant that the fulfillment of the promises of the New Covenant would not depend upon the obedience of Israel. In fact, God indicated that He would fulfill the New Covenant's promises, not because Israel would deserve it, but because of Israel's disobedience. (Showers 2013, 101-102)

Reinforcing Showers' point that the New Covenant is unconditional, we can read in Ezekiel, "But

I had pity for mine holy name, which the house of Israel had profaned among the heathen, whither they went. Therefore, say unto the house of Israel, thus saith the Lord GOD; I do not this for your sakes, O house of Israel, but for mine holy name's sake, which ye have profaned among the heathen, whither ye went" (Ezek. 36:21-22). In spite of their past and future failures, God will accomplish it for them Himself! This would preclude the belief that Israel has been abandoned and subsequently replaced by the Church. Such a notion is contrary to God's faithfulness and the literal meaning of Scripture.

7

Prophecies To Israel

All of the covenants in the previous chapter could be considered prophecies as well. Anything in which God says *I will* could be considered a declaration of future events. In this chapter, we will consider prophecies which are presented as revelation of future events and, in turn, these could be considered promises. It is impossible to understand future prophecies without including the Book of Daniel. The ten tribes of Israel had been dispersed into the nations. The remaining two tribes of Judah had lost possession of the Promised Land and were being punished for their failure to observe the Law. Judah had been carried off into exile in Babylon. Daniel was given the prophecies concerning the fulfillment of the Covenants, specifically the Davidic and Palestinian (Land), while he was in Babylon. The Jews had been waiting for the promised Messiah and the restoration of the Kingdom. These prophecies were to encourage Israel that God had not forgotten them. In familiar verses, Isaiah proclaimed God's promise of their coming King Who would rule over God's creation from Jerusalem:

> For unto us a child is born, unto us a son is given: and the government shall be upon his shoulder: and his name shall be called Wonderful, Counsellor, The mighty God, The everlasting Father, The Prince of Peace.
>
> Of the increase of his government and peace there shall be no end, upon the throne of David, and upon his kingdom, to order it, and to establish it with judgment and with justice from henceforth even for ever. The zeal of the LORD of hosts will perform this. (Isa. 9:6-7).

In this chapter, we will examine the prophecy concerning the Gentiles and Israel, as the Chosen Nation. We have covered the dispensations from the Creation to Moses. They included the Age of Innocence (from Creation to the Fall), the Age of Conscience (from the expulsion to the Flood), the Age of Human Government (the forming of the Nations at the Towel of Babel until Armageddon). The final dispensation already considered is the Age of Law (giving of the Law to the Jews.) It should be noted that the Nations, referred to in the New Testaments as *the Gentiles*, as well as the Jews still exist. We will see in the prophecies that God has a plan for the Gentiles and that plan relates to Israel. Before the creation of the Church, there existed only Jew (Israel) and non-Jew (Gentiles). We will examine Daniel's prophecy concerning the Time of the Gentiles and Israel, as the Chosen Nation.

Some theologians apply an interpretation based upon an allegorical method to prophecies. This makes it extremely difficult to understand as it could be interpreted multiple ways. Our approach going forward will be a literal approach. Perhaps symbols or metaphors are used, but the message is to be understood as plain and normal text. If we read Psalm 22, we can see that much of the first part concerning the death of Christ has been fulfilled. Yet, the promise of the Kingdom has not. J. Dwight Pentecost, another professor from both Dallas Theological Seminary and Philadelphia Bible Institute, writes:

> As the picture of Messiah's death was literally fulfilled it can only be concluded that that which flows

from Messiah's death in fulfillment of the covenants will be literally fulfilled also. It should be obvious that the method used by God to fulfill prophecies that have been fulfilled historically will be His method in the fulfillment of all prophecies. Inasmuch as all prophecies that have been fulfilled have been fulfilled literally, consistency demands that this method must be adopted for those portions of the prophetic Scriptures that, as yet, may be unfulfilled. Since the portions of the Abrahamic covenant that have been fulfilled were fulfilled literally, it would be concluded that the unfulfilled portions will be fulfilled in like manner. (Pentecost1964, 83-84)

It must be agreed that many of the prophecies of the Bible have not yet been fulfilled. This would bring us to the study of the future things to come, eschatology. Here we begin our study by considering the eschatological prophecy of Daniel.

Daniel, a prophet during the Babylonian Exile, encouraged the Jews with his prophecy of the coming Kingdom. He records two visions regarding the future of which we will now consider. It would be worth the reader's time to read the book of Daniel.

The Great Statue

The second chapter of Daniel records the prophecy and interpretation in full. David Yonggi Cho, formerly the pastor of the largest church in the world, offers an interpretation of the great statue:

> Daniel's interpretation that the golden head in the dream was Nebuchadnezzar himself must have been a shock to the king . . .
>
> The inferior kingdom that would arise after Babylon, which is represented by the breast of silver, . . . refers to the coalition kingdom of Media and Persia, which conquered Babylon at the time of Belshazzar. The breast of silver had two arms, representing the two members of the coalition. These two kingdoms alternately ruled what had been the whole region of Babylonia.

The belly of brass followed the breast of silver. This referred to the Greek age of Alexander the Great, who conquered the Medo-Persian kingdom. Babylon and Medo-Persia, which had ruled before the Greek empire, were Asian kingdoms. Alexander the Great, however, arose and conquered Macedonia in Europe, Iran and Syria in western Asia, and Egypt in Africa. He built the Greek empire by uniting the East and the West.

So, the brass that formed the belly extended to the thighs and was divided into two parts because Alexander the Great built a kingdom that extended to the east and the west, which broke the coalition of the Medo-Persian kingdom. One leg refers to the West and the other to the East.

Next came the statue's legs of iron. After the fall of Alexander the Great, the kingdom he had built was divided into four parts by the four gen erals who had been his staff officers. They lasted for only a short period and were conquered by Rome, which arose at that time. And because Rome established a kingdom, the territory that extended to the east and west was represented by the legs of iron.

In addition, the feet and toes were made of both iron and clay. This signified that the kingdom would be divided. Part of it would be strong, and part of it would be weak at the same time . . .

The ten toes of both feet therefore show that ten nations will be somehow united in the former territory of the eastern and western parts of the Roman empire. (Cho 1998, 12-13)

Before the Time of the Gentiles is over and the Lord Jesus Christ subjugates the nations, Rome must be once again reunited. There is conjecture that the ten principal nations comprising the European Union may be the basis of a reunited Roman Empire.

Clarence Larkin, a Baptist pastor, was best known for his talents as a professional draftsman. It was his talent as a draftsman that resulted in numerous graphic illustrations of complex theological truths interpreted from a dispensational point of view. Larkin's chart is titled the Time of the Gentiles which is also called the Time of the Nations (the non-Jews).

The Seventy Weeks

Another prophecy of Daniel concerns Israel and this same period of time. Remember we are dealing with two of the three distinct divisions of people: Jew and Gentile. (The Church, as a distinct group, will be discussed later.) Daniel's vision came in answer to his prayer for Israel. It is important that we include, with comments, the entire text of Daniel concerning the seventy weeks prophecy:

> Seventy weeks are determined upon thy people and upon thy holy city, to finish the transgression, and to make an end of sins, and to make reconciliation for iniquity, and to bring in everlasting righteousness, and to seal up the vision and prophecy, and to anoint the most Holy.

Know therefore and understand, that from the going forth of the commandment to restore and to build Jerusalem unto the Messiah the Prince shall be seven weeks, and threescore and two weeks: the street shall be built again, and the wall, even in troublous times.

And after threescore and two weeks shall Messiah be cut off, but not for himself: and the people of the prince that shall come shall destroy the city and the sanctuary; and the end thereof shall be with a flood, and unto the end of the war desolations are determined. And he shall confirm the covenant with many for one week: and in the midst of the week he shall cause the sacrifice and the oblation to cease, and for the overspreading of abominations he shall make it desolate, even until the consummation, and that determined shall be poured upon the desolate. (Dan. 9:24-27)

Look at this equation: $7 + 62 = 69$. Now, consider the following comparison. Your friend lives exactly 70 miles from your home. You get into your car and drive seven miles and stop to get gas. You get into the car again and drive another sixty-two miles when you pull over at a rest area. Whether you wait one day or a thousand, the results are still the same: there is one more mile left to go before the journey is completed. Remember this fact later when we delve deeper into the seventieth week.

Cho points out, "Because a week is composed of seven days, the term 'seventy weeks' here means seventy times seven days, or four hundred ninety days" An example of when one day equals a year comes from the book of Numbers. Israel rejected the report of the spies about the Promised Land. They were gone for forty days. God was angry for their lack of faith. "After the number of the days in which ye searched the land, even forty days, each day for a year, shall ye bear your iniquities, even [that is to say] forty years, and ye shall know my breach of promise" (Num. 14:34). This is only one example of God making one day worth one year. Therefore, the sixty-nine weeks would be the same as 483 years.

The starting point of the clock, if you will, was the decree. Remember, "Know therefore and understand, that from the going forth of the commandment to restore and to build Jerusalem unto the Messiah the Prince shall be seven weeks, and threescore and two weeks: the street shall be built again, and the wall, even in troublous times" (Dan. 9:25). It is possible to establish that date using Ezra 1:1-4 and Nehemiah chapters one and two. We read in Ezra, "Now in the first year of Cyrus king of Persia, that the word of the LORD by the mouth of Jeremiah might be fulfilled, the LORD stirred up the spirit of Cyrus king of Persia, that he made a proclamation throughout all his kingdom . . ." (v. 1:1). Cho citing research tells us the decree, ". . . was given in the month of Nisan in the twentieth year of King Artaxerxes. Converted to dates on our modern calendar, this corresponds to March 14, 445 B.C." Cho's calculations, which included adjustments for the Hebrew calendar, brought the date that the Messiah would be cut off to April 6, A.D. 32. Sir Robert Anderson, another respected theologian, agreed with this date. However, Larkin calculated that date to be April 2, A.D. 30. These dates are to correspond with the historical date of the Lord's crucifixion–the time Messiah would be cut off and have nothing.

Scripture sometimes uses one verse that may describe two separate historical events. Consider the Scripture Christ read in the synagogue at the beginning of His earthly ministry. He only read half of the verse; then sat down saying, ". . . This day is this scripture fulfilled in your ears" (Lk. 4:21). He read, "To proclaim the acceptable year of the LORD . . ." (Isa. 61:2). To the amazement of those in attendance, He did not read the remainder of the verse, ". . . and the day of vengeance of our God . . ." (v. 2). He did this because that second part of the verse was still yet to come. In Daniel's prophecy we just read, the same is true. "And after threescore and two weeks shall Messiah be cut off, but not for himself . . ." reflects Christ's death on the cross and the end of His earthly mission. Yet the remainder of that verse, " . . . and the people of the prince [Antichrist] that shall come shall destroy the city and the sanctuary; and the end thereof shall be with a flood, and unto the end of the war desolations are determined" (Dan. 9:26). This provides us with evidence that there is a gap. The latter part of the prophecy, the remaining seven years after Messiah is cut off, is dependent upon the arrival of the Antichrist and ends with war desolations.

You may ask, "What is the significance of the Seventy Weeks?" Anderson provides us with a summary:

> The scepter of earthly power which was entrusted to the house of David, was transferred to the Gentiles in the

person of Nebuchadnezzar, to remain in Gentile hands "until the times of the Gentiles be fulfilled."

The blessings promised to Judah and Jerusalem were postponed till after a period described as "seventy weeks"; and at the close of the sixty-ninth week of this era the Messiah should be "cut off."
These seventy weeks represent seventy times seven prophetic years of 360 days, to be reckoned from the issuing of an edict for the rebuilding of the city – "the street and rampart," of Jerusalem.
The edict in question was the decree issued by Artaxerxes Longitmanus in the twentieth year of his reign, authorizing Nehemiah to rebuild the fortifications of Jerusalem.

The date of Artaxerxes's reign can be definitely ascertained - not from elaborate disquisitions by biblical commentators and prophetic writers, but by the united voice of secular historians and chronologers.

The statement of St. Luke is explicit and unequivocal, that our Lord's public ministry began in the fifteenth year of Tiberius Caesar. It is equally clear that it began shortly before the Passover[.] The date of it can thus be fixed as between August A.D. 28 and April A.D. 29. The Passover of the crucifixion therefore was in A.D. 32, when Christ was betrayed on the night of the Paschal Supper, and put to death on the day of the Paschal Feast. (Anderson 2014, 106)

Most denominations have diminished the importance of Israel role in God's grand revelation to Mankind. We will end with Anderson who puts it all in perspective:

If the digression may be pardoned, it may be well to amplify this, and explain my meaning more fully. That Israel will again be restored to the place of privileged and blessing upon the earth is not a matter of opinion, but of faith; and no one who accepts the Scriptures as Divine can question it. Here the language of the Hebrew prophets is unusually explicit. (Anderson 2014, 212)

We can cite Paul's reference to God's unconditional promise to Israel and His faithfulness to them, "I say then, Hath God cast away his people? God forbid. For I also am an Israelite, of the seed of Abraham, of the tribe of Benjamin. God hath not cast away his people which he foreknew . . ." (Rom. 11:1-2a). What, then, is His plan for His Chosen People?

In the next chapter, we will finish the remaining dispensations from Moses–the giving of the Law–until the Messianic Kingdom is established in fulfillment of Daniel's prophecy.

8

The Dispensational System
Part 2

Moses To Eternity

It is at this point where we must diverge from the standard theological position of most dispensationalists. This is not to disparage their contribution to the development of the dispensational system. Concerning principles of interpretation, Anderson writes, ". . . the real question at issue relates to the character, not of individuals, but of a system." The concern is not whether we can agree on the seven dispensations. The question is When does the Church Age begin and end? This is the defining factor in understanding Paul's unique message in view of the other Apostles. It will be our purpose to demonstrate this conclusively.

I have the greatest respect for the biblical scholars which I will cite in the following pages. We have
stepped away from those that have allegorized Israel
in the Old Testament, God's elect, as the Church in
the New Testament. It was shown the New Covenant, examined in a previous chapter, was promised
to Israel. So where does the Church–the Body of
Christ start? The predominant position is Acts 2.
Pentecost has an incredible summary with which I
whole-heartedly agree:

> The church is manifestly an inter-
> ruption of God's program for Israel,
> which was not brought into being
> until Israel's rejection of the offer of
> the Kingdom. It must logically fol-
> low that this mystery program must
> itself be brought to a conclusion be-
> fore God can resume His dealing
> with the nation Israel, as has been
> shown previously He will do. The
> mystery program, which was so dis-
> tinct in its inception, will certainly
> be separate at its conclusion. This
> program must be concluded before
> God resumes and culminates His
> program for Israel. This mystery
> concept of the church makes a pre-

tribulation rapture a necessity. (Pentecost 1964, 201)

However, his position on the beginning of the church is typical of most dispensationalist when he writes, "It was after the rejection of the Cross that the church had its inception in Acts 2." I think this belief is based upon assumption and not facts.

As with all presuppositions, they are based on assumptions that need to be proved. Merrill C. Tenney who was Dean of the Graduate School and professor at Wheaton College, is a well-respected conservative evangelical. Let us demonstrate my point with his position. Using the conditional preface of "if" he writes, "The first period in the history of the early church can be characterized as that of establishment." He adds additional facts, "At the outset there is no evidence that the believers broke sharply with Judaism." Now, he adds a statement which is the "then" resultant, "Pentecost was a Jewish feast before it became a Christian anniversary." Nearly all conservative dispensationalists would concur. He continues, "The preaching of the apostles interpreted the Old Testament Scriptures and stressed Jesus' Messianic office, even avowing that if the nation repented, the Messiah Jesus would return (3:19-20)."

Remember the promise made to the Jews concerning their Messiah in Daniel? If we read Peter's address at Pentecost, only fifty days after the Passover, it is offering the return of their Messiah. Tenney continues, "The addresses of Peter were gauged for a Jewish audience, and so was the great appeal of Stephen. When the apostles went to worship, they went to the temple (3:1), and Stephen debated in the synagogues (6:9-10) of the foreign residents in Jerusalem." This again is the typical representation of the beginnings of the Church. This makes the entire New Testament applicable to the Church; Israel losing its distinction. Throughout the remainder of this chapter, we will present an alternative to this common presupposition. Then, through the following chapters, we will apply a test to this presupposition as to whether it is a cohesive theological system for interpreting the New Testament text.

This method is different from traditional dispensational theology only slightly and, as such, is referred to as *ultradispensational* or *hyperdispensational*. Their analysis is only partially right. Concerning the distinction between Jews who accept the good news about the Messianic Kingdom and the Church–the Body of Christ, Ryrie writes, "Interestingly, ultradispensationalism uses the same argument for two baptisms to support their teaching of two churches within the Acts period. The Petrine church, or Jewish church, existed from Pentecost to Paul, and the body church from Paul on." He goes onto to write, "The Jewish church received power by baptism *in* the Spirit, and the Pauline, or body, church is formed by the baptism *by* the Spirit." He cites Charles F. Baker who holds to this belief. The Jewish Apostles baptized, after a confession, with water. Paul did not baptize with water except in a few cases at the beginning of his ministry.

Ryrie defines *Ultradispensationalism* as follows:

When one boils down the points of agreement and differences between the extreme and moderate schools of ultradispensationalism, he finds one outstanding difference remaining between ultradispensationalism and dispensationalism. It concerns the beginning of the church, the body of Christ. Virtually all ultradispensationalists, of whatever school, agree that it did not begin at Pentecost. All dispensationalists agree that it did. Therefore, ultradispensationalism may be defined, or certainly characterized rather definitively, as the school of interpretation that places more than one dispensation between Pentecost and the end of the church age. (Ryrie 2007, 233)

There are seven dispensations which are common ground between traditional dispensationalist and the, so-called, ultradispensaitonalist. The difference is not an additional dispensation during the Church Age, but a differentiation caused by a parenthetical interlude. In other words, the time of the Gentiles, as disclosed by Daniel, contained 490 years. After 483 years, the clock stopped. Something new happened. However, there is still the remaining seven years known as Jacob's Time of Trouble or, more commonly, the Tribulation. Therefore, contrary to Ryrie's assertion, there is only one dispensation concerning the Church which ends with the Rapture. There follows the final years of the Age of Law or Mosaic Age leading up to the establishment of the Millennial Kingdom, the seventh and final dispensation upon which all dispensationalists would agree. If this is our difference, let us take a closer look at this.

Perhaps we need another way to look at this. Cornelius R. Stam was founder and president of the Berean Bible Society. He offers this approach:

The most important division in the Bible is that between *prophecy* and the great *mystery* proclaimed by the Apostle Paul.

It is a striking fact that the very opening words of the Bible read: "In the beginning God created *the heaven* and *the earth.*" It does not say that He created the universe, but *the heaven* and *the earth*. This is because He had a purpose concerning the earth quite distinct from His purpose concerning heaven. His purpose concerning *the earth* and Christ's reign upon it is the subject of prophecy (II Pet. 1:16-19). His purpose concerning *heaven* and our exaltation there with Christ is the subject of *"the mystery"* (Eph. 2:4- 10; 3:1-4). Into these two great subjects the Bible is basically divided. (Stam 2008, 47-48)

There is a difference between prophecy and mystery. The Mystery of which we speak is one which was hidden by God until He chose to reveal it to Paul. In other words, it is something that we cannot know until we are told. Concerning this mystery, Paul writes:

> Whereof I am made a minister, according to the dispensation of God which is given to me for you, to fulfil the word of God; Even the mystery which hath been hid from ages and from generations, but now is made manifest to his saints: To whom God would make known what is the riches of the glory of this mystery among the Gentiles; which is Christ in you, the hope of glory: Whom we preach, warning every man, and teaching every man in all wisdom; that we may present every man perfect in Christ Jesus: Whereunto I also labor, striving according to his working, which worketh in me mightily. (Col. 1:24-29)

Israel was presented with the Kingdom offer of their Messiah. In a parable, Jesus foretold of their decision to reject their King. ". . . A certain nobleman went into a far country to receive for himself a kingdom, and to return. And he called his ten servants, and delivered them ten pounds, and said unto them, Occupy till I come. But his citizens hated him, and sent a message after him, saying, "We will not have this man to reign over us" (Lk. 19:12-14).

Until Paul, we are told that the *mystery* was hidden. Stam writes:

> When Israel rejected her Messiah, God cast her aside (temporarily) along with the other nations, that He might offer to all His enemies everywhere reconciliation by grace alone, through faith in the rejected Christ. Thus "the dispensation of the grace of God" was ushered in (Eph. 3:2) so that those willing to accept God's grace might be reconciled to Him in one body by the cross (Eph. 2:16). (Stam 2008, 57)

God has concluded both Jews and Gentiles in unbelief. His purpose is that He might be able to show mercy to all. Paul writes, "And that he might reconcile both unto God in one body by the cross, having slain the enmity thereby: And came and preached peace to you [Gentiles] which were afar off, and to them [Israel] that were nigh" (Eph. 2:16-17).

There were two distinct groups of people comprising humanity in the Old Testament–those within the Commonwealth of Israel and those without. Now, Christ has reconciled them both by breaking down the dividing partition within His Body, the Church (*cf.* Eph. 2:11-22). This proves that there is something different in Paul's writings, but is there any proof of the exclusivity of the ministry of Christ, prior to his crucifixion, to the Jews only?

Two references from the Gospels will suffice at least for our purpose here. The first involved a Gentile mother whose daughter was possessed by a demon. She continued to follow Him and would not cease. We read:

> And, behold, a woman of Canaan came out of the same coasts, and cried unto him, saying, Have mercy on me, O Lord, thou son of David; my daughter is grievously vexed with a devil. But he answered her not a word. And his disciples came and besought him, saying, Send her away; for she crieth after us. But he answered and said, I am not sent but unto the lost sheep of the house of Israel.

Then came she and worshipped him, saying, Lord, help me. But he answered and said, It is not meet to take the children's bread, and to cast it to dogs. And she said, Truth, Lord: yet the dogs eat of the crumbs which fall from their masters' table. Then Jesus answered and said unto her, O woman, great is thy faith: be it unto thee even as thou wilt. And her daughter was made whole from that very hour. (Matt. 15:22-28)

The Lord Jesus Christ made it clear to this Gentile woman that He had come specifically for Israel who was lost. He even refers to her as a "dog" and Israel as "the children," but He makes an exception in her case based upon her extraordinary faith.

Our second example involves the Lord Jesus Christ sending out His twelve disciples with the glad-tidings of the Kingdom. We read in Matthew, "These twelve Jesus sent forth, and commanded them, saying, 'Go not into the way of the Gentiles, and into any city of the Samaritans enter ye not: But go rather to the lost sheep of the house of Israel. And as ye go, preach, saying, the kingdom of heaven is at hand'" (vv. 10:5-7). Prior to His ascension He gave

His disciples what many call the Great Commission. "Go ye therefore, and teach all nations, baptizing them in the name of the Father, and of the Son, and of the Holy Ghost: Teaching them to observe all things whatsoever I have commanded you: and, lo, I am with you always, even unto the end of the world. Amen (vv. 28:19-20). They had no new revelation so the Gospel of the Kingdom was being preached. There were requirements too. First, there was necessity of being baptized. Second, He instructed them to observe all the commandments. At this point there had not been a change of message and this message will be the same one preached after the Rapture of the Body of Christ: Jesus of Nazareth is the Christ, the Son of God, the son of David, and Israel's King.

One further example from the Acts of the Apostles involves Pentecost which many attribute as the start of the Church. At the close of Peter's epic speech in which he quotes the prophet Joel and King David, he said, "Therefore let all the house of Israel know assuredly, that God hath made the same Jesus, whom ye have crucified, both Lord and Christ" (Acts 2:26). The crowd which Peter had addressed as "Ye men of Judaea, and all ye that dwell at Jerusalem" (v. 14) had listened intently. "Now when they heard this, they were pricked in their heart, and said unto Peter and to the rest of the apostles, Men and brethren, what shall we do?" (v. 37). Let us consider Peter's response. Did he mention trusting in the blood of the crucified Savior for remission of their sins or the power of the resurrection reconciling them as sinners to a gracious God? No. "Then Peter said unto them, Repent, and be baptized every one of you in the name of Jesus Christ for the remission of sins, and ye shall receive the gift of the Holy Ghost" (v. 38).

Certainly, a comparison has made between the familiar and the new. Ryrie presents his assessment of the *ultradispensaitonalist* view:

> Normative dispensationalists believe that there are some basic errors in the ultradispensational system, and, therefore, they reject the system as diverse from their own and reject any implication that the two are similar . . .
>
> . . . a dispensation has been defined as a distinguishable economy in the outworking of God's purpose. In relation to ultradispensationalism the definition raises this most pertinent question: Is something distinguishably different being done since Paul

came on the scene that was not being done from Pentecost to the time of Paul? (Ryrie 2007, 234)

To this question, we would have to answer with a resounding, "Yes!" There is a difference and we will see it much clearer in the following chapters.

9

The Apostle Paul

What is it about the Apostle Paul that drives so many people, first the Jews then later many Christians, to despise this man? In order to answer that question, we need to examine the man himself, his supernatural calling, and his ministry. We want to fully understand who he is, his life and mission, and his unique message of glad-tidings. William R. Newell, pastor and teacher at Moody Bible Institute under R. A. Torrey, asks, "Is it not strange that of the twenty-eight chapters of Acts, sixteen (seventeen, if we include chapter 9) should be given to that apostle who was not one of the original Twelve at all and was not converted until long after Pentecost? Must there not be a deep reason for this? What is that reason?"

An argument has been made that Paul was supposed to be the intended replacement for Judas who had died. They contend the Lord's disciples, after His resurrection, moved too quickly to replace him. Peter, remembering what the Lord had promised the Twelve, was eager to be fully prepared for the Kingdom's immediate fulfillment. Concerning this, we read, "And Jesus said unto them, Verily I say unto you, That ye which have followed me, in the regeneration when the Son of man shall sit in the throne of his glory, ye also shall sit upon twelve thrones, judging the twelve tribes of Israel" (Matt. 19:28). If we search the text we will find that the requirement for Judas' replacement was something that the Apostle Paul could never have fulfilled. Peter speaking in the Upper Room:

> For it is written in the book of Psalms, Let his habitation be desolate, and let no man dwell therein: and his bishoprick [position of overseer] let another take. Wherefore of these men which have companied with us all the time that the Lord Jesus went in and out among us, Beginning from the baptism of John, unto that same day that he was taken up from us, must one be ordained to be a witness with us of his resurrection. (Acts 1:20-22)

104

Newell writes, "The use of the lot was the Jewish appeal to God and was wholly natural to the Apostles, and it further marks this proceeding as entirely Jewish. We shall see that Matthias completed the Jewish apostolate." Paul could not have met these qualifications. There is no evidence of his connection with the Lord Jesus Christ prior to his conversion. Nevertheless, his conversion presents an interesting and unique encounter with the Living Savior.

Much of the distain for Paul may be the result of his persecution of the new Jewish sect and his involvement as a co-conspirator in the death of Stephen. From a historical perspective there is cause for these emotions. "After the death and burial of Stephen, the persecution still raged in Jerusalem. That temporary protection which had been extended to the rising sect by such men as Gamaliel was now at an end. Pharisees and Sadducees–priests and people–alike indulged the most violent and ungovernable fury. . . The eminent and active agent in this persecution was Saul." With the official endorsement of the Sanhedrin, Paul left Jerusalem en route to Damascus in present day Syria with the purpose of apprehending these infidels and bringing back to Jerusalem to face justice.

Conybeare, a translator of Paul's epistles, and Howson, an expert in historical and geographical data, collaborated to document the life and epistles of Paul. In order to avoid the temptation of overemphasizing the conversion of Paul, we will defer to their opinion. He writes, "If the importance we are intended to attach to particular events in early Christianity is to be measured by the prominence assigned to them in the Sacred Records, we must confess that, next after the Passion of our blessed Lord, the event to which our serious attention is especially called is the Conversion of St. Paul. One would expect that as a late comer to the movement Paul would immediately head to Jerusalem, the headquarters of those awaiting the arrival of the Kingdom. However, Paul heads into Arabia for a meeting with the Lord Himself.

In his letter to the Galatians, Paul writes "But I certify you, brethren, that the gospel which was preached of me is not after man. For I neither received it of man, neither was I taught it, but by the revelation of Jesus Christ" (Gal. 1: 11-12). Explaining the circumstances of this private tutelage, he continues, "But when it pleased God, who separated me from my mother's womb, and called me by his grace, To reveal his Son in me, that I might preach him among the heathen; immediately I conferred not with flesh and blood: Neither went I up to Jerusalem to them which were apostles before me; but I went into Arabia, and returned again unto Damascus" (vv. 15-17).

The perceived importance of Jerusalem on the development of all doctrine was pervasive. All eyes were on ". . . Jerusalem . . . the Holy City of the whole Bible, the place where Jesus was crucified, the place where the Holy Spirit descended on the day of Pentecost, and the place where the Twelve Apostles labored," writes Newell. He continues with the obvious and popular conclusion, "Therefore, it was natural to expect that Jerusalem would be the center from which all the Christian world–that is, those who accepted Jesus as the Messiah–were to be directed and controlled, that Jerusalem would be the only place to look for true doctrine, the Twelve Apostles." However, it was three years before Paul journeyed to Jerusalem. He stayed there fifteen days and saw only Peter and James, the Lord's brother. He continued in his proclamation of the glad-tidings for salvation by grace without works.

After fourteen years, taking Barnabas and Titus with him, he met with the apostles in Jerusalem to confer with them. Speaking to those who appeared to be in charge, they could add nothing of import to his words. The God that had entrusted the glad-tidings to Peter for the circumcised also entrusted Paul with the glad-tidings to uncircumcised. The conference closed with this: "And when James, Cephas, and John, who seemed to be pillars, perceived the grace that was given unto me, they gave to me and Barnabas the right hands of fellowship; that we should go unto the heathen [uncircumcised], and they unto the circumcision" (Gal. 2:9). Having received the right hand of fellowship, the recognition of his unique message to the Gentiles, he continued with his evangelism. In spite of this supposed endorsement by the Council in Jerusalem, Paul continues to defend his position as an apostle. To the Corinthians he writes, "Am I am not an apostle? am I not free? have I not seen Jesus Christ our Lord? (1 Cor. 9:1a).

Donald Guthrie, principal at London Bible College, writes of Paul's importance and influence on the church throughout its history:

> There is no denying that Paul held a high view of apostolic authority. He further regarded apostleship as a special gift from God (Rom. 1:5; Gal. 1:1). His own calling as apostle placed him on an equal footing with

the Jerusalem apostles (*cf.* his argument in Gal. 2). He recognizes that the special qualification of an apostle was that he was a witness to the resurrected Christ and was commissioned by Christ. He claims a revelation which fulfils these conditions (Gal. 1:1, 12). The apostles were entrusted with a missionary task and Paul appeals to his calling as minister to the Gentiles (Rom. 1:Sf.; Gal. 2:8). In his list of specific resurrection appearances in 1 Corinthians 15, Paul includes himself as one 'untimely born' (15:8), which suggests that he was the last. For him apostleship was an office restricted to a definite group and was in no sense an ongoing phenomenon. (Guthrie 1981, 768)

Paul's unique message was centered on the work of the Cross and God's grace in freely offering the substitutionary atonement of His death and the life-changing power of His resurrection. This has led many who oppose Paul to charge those who promulgate his gospel message of "grace alone" or "grace plus nothing" to be antinomians. Antinomianism is the belief that Christians are released by grace from the obligation of observing the moral law. Paul explains that as believers of the Gospel of Grace we have *liberty* but not *license*. Guthrie asserts that this would be a misunderstanding of Paul's message. He writes, "But it would be wrong to suppose that Paul advocates the total abrogation of the law. He is in no sense an antinomian, in spite of all he has said about the end of the law. It is important to note his positive approach on this theme, because of its value in assessing the nature of Christian liberty."

There is a marked distinction comparing Peter's message of the Gospel of the Kingdom and Paul's Gospel of Grace; even how they operated amongst the people. Stam makes a valid comparison:

> "The signs of an apostle" were wrought by Paul, but he did not have the "keys" to the body as Peter did to the kingdom, nor was he given authority to remit sins. Indeed, since baptism "for the remission of sins" had been set aside in favor of justification by grace, through faith, without works, he could have no part in remitting sins except indirectly by proclaiming the glad news. (Stam 2008, 162)

Much of the opposition which Paul faced came from Jewish believers from the Jerusalem converts who had committed to Jesus Christ as their Messiah, but maintained the Jewish traditions including the Law. It was the Lord Jesus Christ that told His disciples, "Think not that I am come to destroy the law, or the prophets: I am not come to destroy, but to fulfil" (Matt. 5:17). These men were called *Judaizers* because of their agenda. They sought to teach these Grace Gospel believers they needed to also submit to the Law and traditions of the Jews. At one point, Paul confronts Peter publicly concerning this matter. Peter had enjoyed the liberty of the Gospel of Grace while among the Gentiles, but when the Jews from Jerusalem arrived, Peter changed his position. He taught, contrary to Paul, that the Christians were still under the Law.

Paul writes, "But when I saw that they [the Gentile Christians] walked not uprightly according to the truth [liberty in Christ] of the gospel, I said unto Peter before them all, If thou, being a Jew, livest after the manner of Gentiles [while amongst them enjoying your liberty in Christ], and not as do the Jews [under the burden of the Law], why compellest thou the Gentiles to live as do the Jews? (Gal. 2:14). Guthrie summarizes this well:

> It is not surprising that many of the
> problems raised by false teachers in

Paul's churches involved a legalistic approach to Christian life (*cf.* Galatians and Colossians. Note also Tit. 3:9; 1 Tim. 1:7; 4:3). It is no more surprising that Paul saw the need to affirm the liberty of the believer in Christ, because he is no longer under law but under grace. (Guthrie 1981, 697)

Therein lies the problem or, as some theologians refer to it as, tension. Two opposing views which are contrary and, in biblical interpretation, this would mean that one of the theological interpretations is wrong due to the lack of harmony in Scripture. How is this to be resolved?

The key is to understanding the *Mystery*. It is a separate and distinct revelation given to the Apostle Paul directly by the Lord Jesus Christ. For dispensational theologians, this new message would mark the beginning of the Age of Grace or, better known as the Church Age.

Compare again Peter's impassioned speech at Pentecost to Israel elicited a response, "Now when they heard this, they were pricked in their heart, and said unto Peter and to the rest of the apostles, Men and brethren, what shall we do?" (Acts 2:37). Peter's response, " . . . Repent, and be baptized every one of you in the name of Jesus Christ for the remission of sins . . ." (v. 38). This response is in line with their message of accepting Jesus Christ as their King in fulfillment of the Davidic prophecy and Jewish baptism as a sign of repentance. It was Israel's repentance as a nation and acknowledgement of her Messiah that would have brought in the Kingdom. However, Israel rejected Him.

On the other hand, Paul presents his message almost from a proprietary perspective and, therefore, must be looked at separately from prophecy. Writing to the Romans, we read:

> Now to him that is of power to stablish you according to *my gospel*, and the preaching of Jesus Christ, according to the *revelation of the mystery*, which *was kept secret* since the world began, But *now is made manifest*, and by the scriptures of the prophets, according to the commandment of the everlasting God, made known to all nations for the obedience of faith: To God only wise, be glory through Jesus Christ for

ever. Amen. (Rom. 16:25-27)

Furthermore, Paul presents himself as a pattern, a model by which others should be compared. As far as the depth of sin could go, Paul argues that, with his persecution of the new believers, he deserved to be named the greatest of all sinners–an enemy of God. Concerning this he writes:

> This is a faithful saying, and worthy of all acceptation, that Christ Jesus came into the world to save sinners; of whom I am chief. Howbeit for this cause I obtained mercy, that in me first Jesus Christ might shew forth all longsuffering, for a pattern [an example to be followed] to them which should hereafter believe on him to life everlasting. (1 Tim. 1:15-16)

How is this new revelation from Paul which is called the *Mystery* to be integrated with the prophecies concerning Israel? Paul makes it clear that the temporary blindness of Israel is ordained until after the fullness of the Time of the Gentiles (Daniel's prophecy), then the completion of the Kingdom promised to Israel will be fulfilled. Paul explains this to the Church–the Body of Christ:

> For I would not, brethren, that ye
> should be ignorant of this mystery,
> lest ye should be wise in your own
> conceits; that blindness in part is
> happened to Israel, until the fullness
> of the Gentiles be come in. And so
> [then] all Israel shall be saved: as it
> is written, There shall come out of
> Sion the Deliverer, and shall turn
> away ungodliness from Jacob: For
> this is my covenant unto them [Is-
> rael], when I [God] shall take away
> their sins. As concerning the gospel
> [of grace], they [Israel] are enemies
> for your sakes: but as touching the
> election, they [Israel] are beloved for
> the father's sake. (Rom. 11:25-28)

Sometimes it seems like oil and vinegar shaken together. How is one to separate it? The answer is that it takes time and diligence in comparing Scripture with Scripture. Paul wrote to Timothy, as a new messenger of the Gospel of Grace, concerning the importance of differentiating the messages between the two dispensations. He wrote, "Study to shew thyself approved unto God, a workman that needeth not to be ashamed, rightly dividing the word of truth" (2 Tim. 2:15). The importance in "rightly dividing the word of truth" cannot be overemphasized. Failure to do so will create a theological conundrum. Stam agrees:

> Because of a failure to recognize the mystery, some have supposed it necessary to alter prophecy to account for the present condition of Israel and the presence of the predominantly Gentile church of this age.
>
> Seeing that the fulfillment of prophecy apparently ceased shortly after the crucifixion of Christ, and realizing that there was still much left to be fulfilled, these [objectors] have supposed that God could not have meant exactly what He said when He prophesied that Christ would sit on the throne of David in Jerusalem as King of Israel. They have supposed that these things must have been intended in a *"spiritual"* sense and so have concluded that Christ is *now* seated on "David's throne" at God's right hand, thus confusing earthly Jerusalem with "the Jerusalem which

is above." They have further concluded that the church of today is
"spiritual" Israel, that heaven is Canaan, etc.

But there is in fact nothing spiritual
about this interpretation of the
Scripture. It is *carnal,* not spiritual,
to fail to take God at His Word and
to seek to explain away difficulties
by arbitrarily altering what has been
plainly written. (Stam 2008, 59-60)

Newell agrees:

The failure or refusal to discern the
Pauline Gospel as a separate and
new revelation and not a "development from Judaism," accounts for
two-thirds of the confusion in many
people's minds today as regards just
what the Gospel is. Paul's Gospel
will suffer no admixture with works
on the one hand or religious pretensions and performances on the other.
It is as simple and clear as the sunlight from heaven. (Newell 2009, 16)

We closed this chapter with these two summaries from both Stam and Newell to point out the importance of consistently applying a system of theology throughout one's interpretation. We established the apparent validity of the dispensational interpretation of Scripture compared to other systems. We discussed the need to adjust the timeframe concerning the beginning of the parenthetical age commonly called the Church Age which centers on Paul's unique message concerning the Church–the Body of Christ. It begins with the conversion of Paul and ends with the Rapture. In the following chapters, we will examine the New Testament, in sections, by applying this system as a test of its validity measured by its comprehensiveness and cohesiveness.

10

The Gospels

We have broken the New Testament into divisions similar to a chiasmus which is used in Hebrew poetry. This is a literary form which uses words, grammatical constructions, or concepts; repeated in a reverse order to form basically an "X" in shape. It has been said that a chiasmus is "the use of bilateral symmetry about a central axis." The symmetrical shape shows the balance of related concepts and creates a cohesive order for the benefit of the reader. Usually with a chiasmus, the center is of greater importance, but concerning the inspired Word, "All scripture is given by inspiration of God, and is profitable for doctrine, for reproof, for correction, for instruction in righteousness" (2 Tim. 3:16).

So, no Scripture is ever excluded. However, we must apply the warning given by Paul to his protégé Timothy in the verse just prior. "Study to shew thyself approved unto God, a workman that needeth not to be ashamed, rightly dividing the word of truth" (v. 15). When I discuss the following with other Christians their first objecting is that the entire Scripture must be observed. However, Paul makes it clear to Timothy that he must correctly divide the Word of Truth as he presents the good news. In other words, all Scripture is profitable, but may not apply in certain circumstances.

An illustration is shown below for understanding the overall direction we will take. You should notice the balance provided by the portions both above and below the center of the chiasmus. It is this balance with its focal point that creates the unique features of this literary form.

A			The Gospels	Offer of the King and Kingdom
	B		Acts of the Apostles	Transition
		C	Pauline Epistles	Revelation of the Mystery
	B'		Hebrews	Transition
A'			Hebrew Epistles & Revelation	King & Kingdom Fulfilled

We have already divided humanity into two groups: Israel and the Nations (Gentiles). However, with the introduction of the Mystery we will see there is a third entity created in God's sovereign plan which comprises both Jew and Gentile alike. Our

120

contention is that prior to the announcement of this Mystery, the Scriptures are concerned with the completing of the Prophecy Program directed towards Israel. We have examined the prophecies concerning the establishment of Israel as a Kingdom. This is not an allegorical but a literal Kingdom. For Israel will have a King who will sit upon the throne of His father David and that King will rule both Jew and Gentile from His throne in Jerusalem.

The Gospel of Matthew opens with the genealogy of Jesus Christ for the purpose of establishing his Davidic descendance. Matthew records Joseph's lineage and the matter concerning the birth of Our Lord from his perspective. It begins with Abraham (Matt. 1: 2), including both David and Solomon (v. 6); then to King Jeconiah (v. 11). God pronounced a curse on this king preventing him from ever establishing the Davidic line again. (*cf.* Jer. 22:24-30) Regardless of Joseph's claim to the throne, he would not have produced a legitimate heir because of this curse.

The Gospel of Luke, on the other hand, records the genealogy of Mary and life from her perspective concerning the birth of Our Savior. Luke records His lineage starting with Mary and works backwards. The line is traced until it returns to the family of

David (vv. 31-32). However, the son of David involved in this genealogy is not Solomon but Nathan. Mary was a member of the House of David and her Son was also a legitimate heir to the House of David– a human heir to the earthly Davidic Kingdom.

Inasmuch as Prophecy is specific to Israel, there is something else. At no point in Paul's writings is the Church–the Body of Christ ever referred to as "sheep." That is something totally unique to Israel. In the Psalms we read, "Know ye that the LORD he is God: it is he that hath made us, and not we ourselves; we are his people, and the sheep of his pasture" (v. 100:3). The Messiah is referred to as their Shepherd. Repetition is the necessary mother of learning. So, to further prove His Sovereign prerogative whereby He was dealing exclusively with Israel at this time, we turn again to the Gospel of Matthew. "And, behold, a woman of Canaan [a Gentile] . . . cried unto him, saying, Have mercy on me, O Lord, thou son of David; my daughter is grievously vexed with a devil" (v. 15:22). Pay attention to His response for we all know that Jesus healed many people. "But he answered her not a word" (v. 23a). Apparently, she was becoming quite a nuisance and the disciples intervened. "And his disciples came and besought him, saying, Send her away; for she crieth after us" (v. 23b). Is it not odd that the Savior would not answer her? We find out the reason why with His response, "But he answered and said, I am not sent but unto the lost sheep of the house of Israel" (v. 24). Here, again, is the word "sheep" used and, without any doubt, it is being used exclusively for Israel!

A similar situation is recorded for us in the Gospel of John. Again, it concerns Gentiles and Jesus completely ignores them. His response is to His disciples and is foretelling concerning the importance of His impending crucifixion. We read:

> And there were certain Greeks among them that came up to worship at the feast: The same came therefore to Philip, which was of Bethsaida of Galilee, and desired him, saying, Sir, we would see Jesus. Philip cometh and telleth Andrew: and again Andrew and Philip tell Jesus. And Jesus answered them, saying, The hour is come, that the Son of man should be glorified. Verily, verily, I say unto you, Except a corn of wheat fall into the ground and die, it abideth alone: but if it die, it bringeth forth much fruit. (Jn. 12:20-24)

This would indicate that the Christ must die according to God's eternal plan. His sacrifice may be beneficial to more than the Jews alone, such as those that accept the Kingdom Gospel during the time of the Tribulation. During which time those that are following the instructions known as the Great Commission will make known the Gospel of the Kingdom. However, the details of His plan for the Gospel of Grace were yet a mystery and not outlined or made know until His revelation to the Apostle Paul.

We will consider three interpretations of Our Lord's words in the tenth chapter of the Gospel of John. Jesus said, "I am the good shepherd: the good shepherd giveth his life for the sheep" (v.11). Most would believe that, since the Savior died for us, we are also His sheep. This would be a dispensational mistake. Although the Savior did die for our sins, we must pay close attention to whom He was speaking since the church could not have begun until, at least, His resurrection. The contention concerns the following verse. "I am the good shepherd, and know my sheep, and am known of mine. As the Father knoweth me, even so know I the Father: and I lay down my life for the sheep. And other sheep I have, which are not of this fold: them also I must bring, and they shall hear my voice; and there shall be one fold, and one shepherd" (vv. 14-16). The question is Who are the "other" sheep?

I was in a men's study group and the leader offered the following explanation from the commentary in the NIV Study Bible which I will quote here. "The 'other' sheep were non-Jews. Jesus came to save Gentiles as well as Jews. This is an insight into His worldwide mission–to die for the sins of the world. People tend to want to restrict God's blessings to their own group, but Jesus refuses to be limited by the fences we build." This would be a common interpretation unless dispensationally considered. If the Church, the Body of Christ, is never referred to as "sheep" and Scripture states it remained a mystery until later revealed to Paul, who are these "other sheep" to which Our Lord is referring?

One interpretation has to do with the separation of the twelve tribes. The Northern Kingdom under Jeroboam included ten tribes and was known as Israel. The Southern Kingdom under Rehoboam included the two tribes of Benjamin and Judah. As they possessed Jerusalem, the God-appointed capitol, they were considered the "true" Israel. Paul Sadler, president of the Berean Bible Society, writes:

> Consequently, some believe that the
> "other sheep" are the ten northern

tribes who will be brought back into the fold at the Second Coming of Christ. Hence, there will be one fold and one Shepherd. We surely concur that there will be reunification of the tribes of Israel . . . Israel is the sheep of God, whether they were of the northern or southern tribes. The Lord would have never called His *chosen people* the "other sheep." They are *the sheep* and, therefore, the *primary* fold. (Sadler 1995, 66-67)

The correct interpretation has something do to with the Last Days outlined in the Genesis. God spoke to Abraham, "And I will make of thee a great nation, and I will bless thee, and make thy name great; and thou shalt be a blessing: And I will bless them that bless thee, and curse him that curseth thee: and in thee shall all families *of the earth* be blessed" (vv. 12:2-3). The Prophecy Program is indivisible concerning the promises and their fulfillment. These apply solely to Israel and the Gentiles who remain on earth during the Tribulation. The key is these pertain *to the earth*. We must interpret Scripture in light of that fact.

The Gospel of Matthew provides prophecy for

the Last Days as Our Lord teaches and answers His disciples' questions. "When the Son of man shall come in his glory, and all the holy angels with him, then shall he sit upon the throne of his glory [on earth]: And before him shall be gathered all nations: and he shall separate them one from another, as a shepherd divideth his sheep from the goats: And he shall set the sheep on his right hand, but the goats on the left" (vv. 25:13-33). We must not assume that the "goats" are all non-Jews and the meaning is made plain in the remaining verses. Furthermore, this is relative to the First Resurrection which includes Israel and those who were kind to Israel during the time of Jacob's Trouble–the seven years of the Tribulation. The following may explain the "other sheep" who could enter His sheep fold (His *earthly* Kingdom).

> Then shall the righteous answer him, saying, Lord, when saw we thee an hungred, and fed thee? or thirsty, and gave thee drink? When saw we thee a stranger, and took thee in? or naked, and clothed thee? Or when saw we thee sick, or in prison, and came unto thee? And the King shall answer and say unto them, Verily I say unto you, Inasmuch as ye have

done it unto one of the least of these my brethren, ye have done it unto me. (vv. 37-40)

The Church–the Body of Christ is never judged based upon its works relative to salvation. Here the division is made between those Gentiles which aided Israel in her time of need and those that made her tribulation more difficult.

One thing that distinguishes the Church–the Body of Christ from Israel is the Rapture. A unique attribute to the Rapture is its imminence. This is not true concerning the Great Tribulation. Do any of the Gospels teach the Rapture? We will examine at two portions of Scripture that many contend teach the Rapture. Our first will be the portion of the Gospel of Matthew known as the Olivet Discourse where Jesus is alone with his disciples. "And as he sat upon the Mount of Olives, the disciples came unto him privately, saying, Tell us, when shall these things be? and what shall be the sign of thy coming, and of the end of the world?" (Matt 24:3). These questions followed His statement concerning the temple being destroyed. He makes a statement about the Antichrist, "For many shall come in my name, saying, I am Christ; and shall deceive many" (v. 5). He speaks further of false prophets and iniquity abounding, but then makes an odd statement. Speaking to His disciples, prior to His death burial, and resurrection, "And this *gospel of the kingdom* shall be preached in all the world for a witness unto all nations; and *then shall the end come*" (v.14, emphasis mine). What is this Gospel of the Kingdom? Notice the temporal reference. This must relate to the last days of the Tribulation as it immediately precedes the end.

When Jesus sent out His twelve with a message concerning the Kingdom, let us note to whom that message was to be carried. Scripture enumerates His twelve disciples and continues, "These twelve Jesus sent forth, and commanded them, saying, Go not into the way of the Gentiles, and into any city of the Samaritans enter ye not: But go rather to the lost sheep of the house of Israel. And as ye go, preach, saying, The kingdom of heaven is at hand" (vv. 5-7). This appears to be a message intended exclusively for the children of Israel.

Returning to our discussion on the Rapture and its unique connection with the Church, the Body of Christ, we will examine another common Scripture in the gospels which many erroneously apply to the Rapture. This concerns the verses in Matthew where Our Lord compares the Last Days to the Days of Noah. We all know the evil that was rampant prior to the Flood causing God to judge the earth's inhabitants. Its sudden and unexpected occurrence bears another similarity to the Second Coming. Concerning this we read: "Then shall two be in the field; the one shall be taken, and the other left. Two women shall be grinding at the mill; the one shall be taken, and the other left" (Matt: 24: 40-41). A popular belief would be that the ones taken are the ones that have been raptured and those that remain are left to face the horrors of the Tribulation. Concerning this, Sadler writes, "Please bear with me for a moment, but I must ask an elementary question: Who was removed from the earth in Noah's day–was it the believers or the unbelievers? The Genesis record plainly states that the *unbelievers* were swept away to a watery grave." Again, Our Lord is teaching His disciples concerning the Time of Jacob's Trouble. It is the faithful that will stay and the evil ones that will be taken away.

Perhaps the greatest confusion comes from the assumption that the Gospels are written for the benefit of the "Church." Sadler writes, "When *tradition* speaks, Christians bow in humble adoration without regard to the Word, rightly divided." He goes on to make an important point, "One of the rules of hermeneutics (science or interpretation) states: Your conclusion is only as sound as your premise. In other words, if you premise is incorrect, your conclusion, as convincing as it may be, is also *wrong*."

11

The Book of Acts

The book called the Acts of the Apostles is a pivotal book in the New Testament. Without proper dispensational interpretation, one would be oblivious to the shift in paradigm. This being such a critical book in our argument, we must first look at the popular or "traditional" interpretation which is prevalent in most evangelical churches. This would include an examination of their proof texts and interpretations.

The allegorical interpretation teaches that God's elect were considered the Church which consisted of the disciples who were empowered at Pentecost to grow the Church. Others teach the Church began at Pentecost. If that is the case, then it makes the position that the Gospels were written for the Church unsustainable. Israel is and always will be God's chosen people and heirs to the promises and prophecies. For those that believe the Church started in Acts 2, it is presented as the prototype for the modern-day Church. Stam writes:

> Nearly all writers on Acts have assumed, without the slightest foundation, that it is the record of the birth and growth of the Church of this dispensation; that in Acts we find the doctrine and practice of the Church in its earliest and purest form; that it is a spiritual story book containing inspiring examples of what we might do if we but possessed the faith of the first century believers. (Stam 2010, xvii-xviii)

Charles Hodge holds a "traditional" interpretation. The seeds of the Church are planted in the Gospels by the incarnate Savior with His assembling of the twelve disciples. They are told to wait before beginning their Great Commission until they receive power from on high. It is at this point in which the Church actually begins. Concerning this, Hodge writes:

> [Jesus Christ] forbade them to enter upon their office as teachers until

they were endued with power from on high . . . This promise was fulfilled on the day of Pentecost, when the Spirit descended upon the apostles as a mighty rushing wind, and they were filled with the Holy Ghost and began to speak as the Spirit gave them utterance . . . From this moment they were new men, with new views, with new spirit, and with new power and authority. The change was sudden. It was not a development. It was something altogether supernatural . . . Nothing can be unreasonable than to ascribe to mere natural causes this sudden transformation of the apostle from narrrow-minded, bigoted Jews into enlightened, large-minded, catholic Christians. (Hodge 1997, 81-82)

It will be our argument in that the book of Acts is transitional. It moves from the Prophecy Program for Israel to the Mystery Program for the Body of Christ which will be preached by Paul himself. Hodge acknowledges this fact but, the majority of Christendom ignores or simply overlooks it completely. Hodge writes, "Paul pronounces anathema even an angle from heaven who should preach any other gospel than that which he [Paul] had taught (Gal. 1:8)." Stam agrees with our supposition:

> If the Book of Acts truly constitutes "*a pattern of Christian testimony, missionary effort, world evangelism and building of Christian churches–a pattern which we would do well to follow,*" why does no one consistently follow "this holy pattern"? One reason is that no one today *can* follow it. God has rendered this impossible, and all attempts to use Acts as a pattern end in confusion and frustration. (Stam 2010, xviii-xix)

It is this critical difference in the interpretation of the New Testament that is the cause for the misunderstanding and failure of the Church–the Body of Christ to carry out its mission. That mission is outlined in the Pauline epistles which we will examine later. The remainder of this chapter will be devoted to presenting evidence to support our position.

If the traditional interpretation which puts the beginning of the Church at Pentecost, in Chapter 2, then examining the first public presentation of the Gospel following the empowerment of the Holy

Spirit should be our model. We are told that they were obedient to His instructions to stay in Jerusalem and wait; when, suddenly there was a rushing of wind and all those therein were filled with the Holy Spirit. This event did not escape the notice of the multitude without. The text lists foreigners in Jerusalem for the holiday each hearing in his own native language. All of whom sought to understand the meaning of this spectacle; some even suggesting that these anointed believers were drunk. Interestingly, at this point in the narrative, we are told that this was in fulfillment of the prophecy made by Joel. To whom was this prophecy given? It was given to the nation of Israel!

I think it is important to read the entire prophecy to confirm this in the text and view the historical context:

> And it shall come to pass afterward, that I will pour out my spirit upon all flesh; and your sons and your daughters shall prophesy, your old men shall dream dreams, your young men shall see visions: And also upon the servants and upon the handmaids in those days will I pour out my spirit. And I will shew won-

ders in the heavens and in the earth, blood, and fire, and pillars of smoke. The sun shall be turned into darkness, and the moon into blood, before the great and terrible day of the LORD come. And it shall come to pass, that whosoever shall call on the name of the LORD shall be delivered: for in mount Zion and in Jerusalem shall be deliverance, as the LORD hath said, and in the remnant whom the LORD shall call. (Joel 2:28-32)

If this Pentecostal phenomenon is to be attributed to this prophecy, then the later portion must clearly be associated with the final days of the Tribulation which is referred to as the testing of Israel or Jacob's Time of Trouble.

We can almost see the crowd settling down as Peter motions for silence. He begins by addressing them:

Ye men of Israel, hear these words; Jesus of Nazareth, a man approved of God among you by miracles and wonders and signs, which God did by him in the midst of you, as ye yourselves also know: Him, being delivered by the determinate counsel and foreknowledge of God, ye have taken, and by wicked hands have crucified and slain: Whom God hath raised up, having loosed the pains of death: because it was not possible that he should be holden of it. (vv. 2: 22-24)

Then Peter brings to their attention many facts which would only be pertinent to the heirs of the promises of Abraham and David:

For David speaketh concerning him, I foresaw the Lord always before my face, for he is on my right hand, that I should not be moved: Therefore did my heart rejoice, and my tongue was glad; moreover also my flesh shall rest in hope: Because thou wilt not leave my soul in hell, neither wilt thou suffer thine Holy One to see corruption. Thou hast made known to me the ways of life; thou shalt make me full of joy with thy countenance. Men and brethren, let me freely speak unto you of the patriarch David, that he is both dead and buried, and his sepulcher is with us unto this day. Therefore being a prophet, and knowing that God had sworn with an oath to him, that of the fruit of his loins, according to the flesh, he would raise up Christ to sit on his throne; He seeing this before spake of the resurrection of Christ, that his soul was not left in hell, neither his flesh did see corruption. This Jesus hath God raised up, whereof we all are witnesses.

Therefore being by the right hand of God exalted, and having received of the Father the promise of the Holy Ghost, he hath shed forth this, which ye now see and hear. For David is not ascended into the heavens: but he saith himself, The Lord said unto my Lord, Sit thou on my right hand, Until I make thy foes thy footstool. Therefore let all the house of Israel know assuredly, that God hath made the same Jesus, whom ye have crucified, both Lord and Christ. (vv. 2 25-36)

We can be sure that the Word of God always accomplishes its purpose. The Jews who were present for this speech knew very well the Scriptures concerning the promises and prophecies and, therefore, it engendered an immediate response. "Now when they heard this, they were pricked in their heart, and said unto Peter and to the rest of the apostles, Men and brethren, what shall we do?" (v. 37). Pay close attention to Peter's response to their question as we wait to hear him profess the importance of the Christ, their Anointed One, and His death, burial and, most importantly, His resurrection. "Then Peter said unto them, Repent, and be baptized every one of you in the name of Jesus Christ for the remission of sins . . ." (v. 38). What? This should be a disappointment for those professing this as the model Church. If the preceding verse is not enough to make even the staunchest theologian sit up and take notice of the facts presented, the following should. Remember the Children of Israel and how God deals with them as a group whereas the Body of Christ is dealt with on an individual basis for salvation. Peter adds, "For the promise is unto you, and to your children . . ." (v. 39).

A tremendous number of Jews were baptized and accepted the Lord Jesus Christ as their Messiah and King. Some of the characteristics particular to this period of time included repentance and baptism by water, fellowshipping together, the breaking of bread and praying. Another aspect relates to their material possessions: having all things common; they sold their possessions and goods, and distributed them as each one had need. Furthermore, it is pointed out in the text they were ". . . continuing daily with one accord in the temple . . ." (v.46). There was no change in either their tradition or their observance of the Law since they were still children of Abraham. They had, however, acknowledged that their Promised One was indeed the same Jesus of Nazareth Whom they had crucified.

It is important to know that the Greek word translated "church" can be applied to any group or subset of people and is best translated as "assembly". We will cite several examples. In the next verse "And the Lord added to the church daily such as should be saved" (v. 47) the word "church" applies to the group of Jews following the Kingdom Gospel. To the Lord's question "Who do you say that I am?" Peter replied, "Thou art the Christ, the Son of the living God." To which the Lord Jesus said, ". . . and upon this rock [this doctrinal affirmation of faith] I will build my church . . ." (Matt. 16:18). In a completely different context, this same word "church" was used to refer to the riotous public assembly in Ephesus

(Acts. 19:32). To differentiate, Paul includes the phrase "the Body of Christ" in conjunction with the word "church." Finally, "church" is used of the seven churches in Revelation which would refer to a synagogue or a group of believing Jews. In the case of Revelation, the Church–The Body of Christ has already been translated into Heaven according to those who believe in the Rapture. Its righteousness is that of the Christ. It is He Who has made it spotless and without wrinkle. As such, it cannot be judged as can the Jews and Gentiles.

We continue our argument that the initial portion of the book of Acts is a continuation of the Kingdom offered in the Gospels. Stam agrees:

> The only difference between the apostles' position in the four Gospels and in early Acts was that which prophesied events had brought about. In early Acts the resurrection of the crucified King had become the burden of their message and the Spirit had come in power to confirm their testimony. Indeed, the kingdom which these apostles had proclaimed "at hand" during the Lord's earthly ministry, could now be of-

fered (3:19-21). (Stam 2010, xxi)

One of the saying of our Lord Jesus Christ had puzzled me for a long time. He was speaking to the Jews and it concerned what He called the "unpardonable sin:

> Wherefore I say unto you, All manner of sin and blasphemy shall be forgiven unto men: but the blasphemy against the Holy Ghost shall not be forgiven unto men. And whosoever speaketh a word against the Son of man, it shall be forgiven him: but whosoever speaketh against the Holy Ghost, it shall not be forgiven him, neither in this world, neither in the world to come. (Matt. 12:31-32)

Israel rejected the Kingdom offer made by Stephen. They blasphemed against the Holy Spirit who had filled Stephen. The consequences thereof ultimately resulted in the destruction of Jerusalem and Israel's Diaspora forty years later. "The primary question in early Acts, then, is: What will the *nation Israel,* her *government,* her *rulers,* do about Christ?" We will examine this final offer in detail as it marks the pivotal point in the narrative which I previously

144

mentioned.

We are introduced to Stephen in Acts 6. The Kingdom Church was growing and this resulted in a need for those who would serve the needs of this fellowship. Among this group "... they chose Stephen, a man full of faith and of the Holy Ghost" (v. 5) and the evidence of his character was recorded, "And Stephen, full of faith and power, did great wonders and miracles among the people" (v. 8). He spoke boldly and, as a result stirred up the ire of the Jewish ruling council to which they brought Stephen before them along with false witnesses. An important fact to support the anointing of Stephen, "And all that sat in the council, looking steadfastly on him, saw his face as it had been the face of an angel" (v. 15). Interesting! Consider this: the word "angel" means "messenger."

The full account is recorded in Acts chapter 7 and we will only make remarks upon it. Stephen's speech is a recapitulation of the history of God's grace and Israel's continued rebellion. Towards the end, Stephen must have been looking at the reaction on the faces of his audience as he changed his demeanor. Apparently, it became evident that the rulers would reject any appeal Stephen had hoped to make, and he sensed that they would not listen much longer, for suddenly the tone of his message changes. Rather than an appeal there is a stinging indictment. He seems to disown them as he changes his repeated "our fathers" to "your fathers," and charges them with resisting the Holy Spirit, betraying and murdering Christ and despising Moses and the law which they pretended to uphold. In his indictment Stephen went backward from their sin against the Spirit, to that against Christ, to that against Moses and the law, for the effect it would have upon them. Actually their sin against the Spirit was that which sealed their doom.

Though Stephen had stood before them filled with the Holy Spirit and supernaturally transformed as he dealt with them, they would not listen. They had there and then resisted the Holy Spirit and committed the unpardonable sin of which our Lord had so solemnly warned them.

It is at this very point we are introduced to Paul, who at that time was known as Saul, as he was present at the stoning of Stephen. We can assume that he was one in authority as it is recorded that ". . . Saul was consenting unto his death. And at that time there was a great persecution against the church which was at Jerusalem; and they were all scattered . . ." (v. 8:1). This continued for some time as shown in chapter 9, "And Saul, yet breathing out threatenings and slaughter against the disciples of the Lord . . ." (v. 9:1).

It is no doubt due to Paul's initial persecution of these new believers of the Kingdom Gospel that the present church has such as aversion to him and, for that reason, they ignore or discount his inspired revelation. However, as we will show later, it was this flawed man who later wrote Timothy and referred to himself as the chief of sinners (*cf.* 1 Tim. 1:15). This same man who wreaked havoc on the church of Kingdom believers was about to have a cataclysmic confrontation with the risen Lord Jesus Christ Himself. It is recorded in the narrative the details of Paul's conversion on the Road to Damascus. Paul was a representative of the self-righteous and pious Jews in control of the nation of Israel's destiny. Here we must pay careful attention as we are seeing, at this point, the change in dispensations from the Law to that of the Grace of God of which Paul will become the prototype. Later Paul, acknowledging his former deeds, writes: "For I am the least of the apostles, that am not meet [worthy] to be called an apostle, because I persecuted the church of God" (1 Cor. 15:9).

It is interesting to note the discussion between

God and Ananias. God instructs Ananias to go to Paul but he is hesitant knowing the threats that Paul has been making to the believers. God responds with a foreshadowing of the unique nature of Paul ministry, "But the Lord said unto him, Go thy way: for he is a chosen vessel unto me, to bear my name before the Gentiles, and kings, and the children of Israel . . ." (v. 9:15).

The book of Acts records the history of God's work after the resurrection and, therefore extends over a long period of time. Our purpose was to highlight the distinctions between Israel and the Church– the Body of Christ. It has been said that Acts is not a book of doctrine but rather an historical book recording the rejection of the Kingdom offered to Israel according to the prophecy. This does not mean that at this point Israel was completely cast aside. However, their place of prominence in the current dispensation has been replaced temporarily until the Time of the Gentiles should be fulfilled. Luke, the author of the book of Acts, wrote is his Gospel, "And they shall fall by the edge of the sword, and shall be led away captive into all nations: and Jerusalem shall be trodden down of [by] the Gentiles, until the times of the Gentiles be fulfilled" (Lk. 21:24). Luke also writes in the closing lines of the book of Acts, "Be it known therefore unto you, that the salvation of God is sent unto the Gentiles, and that they will hear it. And when he had said these words, the Jews departed, and had great reasoning among themselves" (Acts 28:28-29)

The Kingdom promised to the Jews has been rejected and the proof being their dispersion in A.D. 70 with the destruction of Jerusalem. There is, however, a prevalent belief which is widely held among evangelical churches holding to an allegorical interpretation which was previously discussed. By comparing the allegorical view with what has been developed so far, one can see the distinct contrast. The dispensationalist believes in the literal Davidic throne in Jerusalem. Allegorists contend that Christ is currently ruling from His throne in heaven over His Kingdom. Hodge provides us with his observation concerning what he calls "Christ's visible kingdom":

> As religion is essentially spiritual, an inward state, that aspect of the kingdom of Christ which consists of the truly regenerated is not a visible body, except so far as goodness renders itself visible by its outward manifestations. Nevertheless, as Christ has enjoined upon His people duties which render it necessary that

they should organize themselves in an external society, it follows that there is and must be a visible kingdom of Christ in the world. Christians are required to associate for public worship, for the administration of the sacraments, for the maintenance and propagation of the truth. They therefore form themselves into churches and collectively constitute the visible kingdom of Christ on earth, consisting of all who profess the true religion, together with their children. (Hodge 1997, 407)

If this is true, then the Church, as we know it today, has replaced Israel thereby earning it the title "replacement theology" and the promises which God made exclusively to Israel have been transferred to the Church making His promises to Israel null and void. However, this is not consistent with the truth as outlined within Scripture. We will see in our analysis of the Pauline epistles that Israel will not be cast away as some believe. It is only for a season until they finally repent of their rejection of the Messiah and accept the Lord Jesus Christ as their rightful King.

12

The Pauline Epistles

We must refer back to the diagram which shows the New Testament as a chiasmus. As such, the Pauline Epistles are the focal point. These epistles concern the revelation of the Mystery which was given to Paul and, as such, they are part of God' progressive revelation. God chose to reveal His plan for the Plan of Promise to Abraham, the Plan of Law to Moses, and the Plan of Grace to Paul. Each of these listed are separate and distinct dispensations. The latter, concerning the Age of Grace, was never prophesied in the Old Testament. Although God has always dealt with humankind based upon His grace, His unmerited favor. The revelation to Paul known as "The Mystery" is based solely upon the righteousness of our Lord and Savior Jesus Christ. It was His work alone that can save us.

The word "mystery" (Gr. musterion) as used in

Paul's writings is somewhat unique to his epistles. It is defined in The New Analytical Greek Lexicon as "a matter to the knowledge of which initiation is necessary; a secret which would remain such but for revelation." Introducing the Mystery as a unique concept to Pauline doctrine early in the chapter will allow us to spend the remainder defending it and well as explaining the ramifications it has on this present dispensation.

Before we start, I would like to deal with two objections I received from fellow evangelical Christians with whom I shared these concepts. First, in a chiasmus, the central point is the most important, but this does not to diminish the value of Scripture as a whole. It is the central point because it applies to our present dispensation. However, we do not exclude other Scripture as being worthless, but not all Scripture is applicable to this present dispensation of Grace. Paul instructs Timothy, "All scripture is given by inspiration of God, and is profitable for doctrine, for reproof, for correction, for instruction in righteousness: That the man of God may be perfect, thoroughly furnished unto all good works" (2 Tim. 3:16-17). He also began by informing Timothy that it was important to apply Scripture to whom it was written, "Study to shew thyself approved unto God, a workman that needeth not to be ashamed, rightly dividing the word of truth" (2 Tim. 2:15). Paul is telling Timothy that he must rightly apportion the Scripture to those to whom it is applicable.

Second, the nature of the "mystery" is something requiring a special knowledge and I was falsely accused of promoting "Gnosticism." Satan is a master at counterfeiting. This should not be confused with the rival Greek mystery religions prevalent during the first century. These involved secret ceremonies known only to those initiated into the cult. In order to accept the Lord Jesus Christ, what He did for you and His offer of salvation to you would require special knowledge, but this knowledge is available to all who will listen. Unless it was revealed, it would be impossible to accept. Paul's Gospel of Grace is a unique offer never presented before because it was kept secret. Paul writes in his letter to Romans, "Now to him that is of power to stablish you according to my gospel, and the preaching of Jesus Christ, according to the revelation of the mystery, which was kept secret since the world began." (Rom. 16:25).

It may help by considering two boundary markers for the Church–the Body of Christ and the Dispensation of the Grace of God. The first one would be the conversion of Paul. The other will be the Rapture of the Church–the Body of Christ. Beyond this last marker, the Dispensation of Law resumes for seven years and that will end with the Second Coming of the Messiah, the King of Israel. During the present dispensation, it appears as if God has abandoned us. There are no miracles comparable to those in the Old Testament. It would appear that God is silent. Anderson provides an excellent answer for this:

> Men point to the sad incidents of human life on earth, and they ask "Where is the love of God?" God points to that Cross as the unreserved manifestation of love so inconceivably infinite as to answer every challenge and silence all doubt forever. And that Cross is not merely the public proof of what God has accomplished; it is the earnest [down payment] of all that He has promised. The crowning mystery of God is Christ, for in Him "are all the treasures of wisdom and knowledge hidden." (Anderson 2011, 150)

This is the magnificence of the Gospel of Grace which we will now examine beginning with a look at the messenger. How did he receive this revelation and what makes it so unique?

Paul was called and set apart from the other apostles. Some may think his pragmatic personality is offensive, but to go against the torrent of traditional legalism of the Jewish religion, it was necessary. Stam writes, "Paul said that he was set apart for this from his very birth; every step of his life had led up to this, every step in his life had prepared him for the great ministry that God was to give him." Writing to the Galatians, Paul explains that he did not receive the revelation from any person nor did first he go Jerusalem to be taught by the other apostles with whom the Lord Jesus had spent his earthly ministry. It was three years before he went up to Jerusalem.

> But when it pleased God, who separated me from my mother's womb, and called me by his grace, To reveal his Son in me, that I might preach him among the heathen; immediately I conferred not with flesh and blood: Neither went I up to Jerusalem to them which were apostles before me; but I went into Arabia, and returned again unto Damascus.
>
> Then after three years I went up to

Jerusalem to see Peter, and abode with him fifteen days. But other of the apostles saw I none, save James the Lord's brother. Now the things which I write unto you, behold, before God, I lie not. (Gal. 1:15-20)

We must ask from Whom did Paul receive this revelation? Paul gives us the answer in Galatians. "But I certify you, brethren, that the gospel which was preached of me is not after man. For I neither received it of man, neither was I taught it, but by the revelation of Jesus Christ" (vv. 1:11-12). No longer was Paul seen as the murderer and blasphemer. Stam writes, "The Beloved Son had been rejected but God postponed the day of judgment and instead revealed Christ in matchless grace, through the conversion of the chief of sinners." This created the beginning boundary mark for the beginning of the Age of Grace. What distinguishes this dispensation is the message–the revelation called The Mystery.

Pay close attention to the verb "is" in the following Scripture. Remember that this verb is a verb of equality. The boy *is* Tom. This sentence defines specifically who the boy *is*. Therefore, Tom and "the boy" are one in the same. Paul writes to the Colossians:

If ye continue in the faith grounded and settled, and be not moved away from the hope of the gospel . . . whereof I Paul am made a minister; Who now rejoice in my sufferings for you, and fill up that which is behind of the afflictions of Christ in my flesh for his body's sake, which is the church: Whereof I am made a minister, according to the dispensation of God which is given to me for you, to fulfil the word of God; [That is to say] the **mystery** which hath been hid from ages and from generations, but now is made manifest to his saints: To whom God would make known what is the riches of the glory of this **mystery** among the Gentiles; **which is Christ in you, the hope of glory.** (Col. 1:23-27, emphasis mine)

The importance of that statement is that our *hope is in Christ; Christ is in us and our hope of glory.* No other dispensation could make that claim!

Our examination of the biblical texts concerning Paul and his message are necessarily limited due to our general purpose. Knowing that we are to search the Scriptures to see if what is being said is so, Stam makes a point concerning this:

> It should be evident, even from a superficial reading of the epistles of Paul, that his great message was nothing less than the revelation of a secret "hid in God" all through the preceding dispensations; that what he ushered in was not a fulfillment of the prophetic plan but an *interruption* of it.

> Had Israel accepted Messiah at Pentecost and become the channel of blessing to the nations, men would have witnessed the fulfillment of *prophecy* among the Gentiles, but the present blessing of the Gentiles by grace, through Israel's *fall,* is called a *"Mystery,"* an unprophesied work "among the Gentiles," and . . . God would have His saints know *"what is the riches of the glory of this Mystery among the Gentiles."* God hasten the day when greatly increased numbers will come into the knowledge and blessing of this wonderful truth!

(Stam 2002, 89-90)

The way I like to display it graphically is with the following chart. You can see the similarity in these two dispensations.

	Giver	Intermediary	Recipients
Law→	God→	Moses→	Jews (and Gentiles)
Grace→	God→	Paul→	Gentiles (and Jews)

The battle between salvation by works (the Law) and salvation by grace through faith (Grace) rages on. However, Paul makes it plain, "For by grace are ye saved through faith; and that not of yourselves: it is the gift of God: Not of works, lest any man should boast" (Rom 2:8-9). He further develops the theme concerning this critical doctrine:

> Therefore by the deeds of the law there shall no flesh be justified in his sight: for by the law is the knowledge of sin. But now the right-eousness of God without the law is manifested, being witnessed by the law and the prophets; Even the

righteousness of God which is by faith of Jesus Christ unto all and upon all them that believe: for there is no difference: For all have sinned, and come short of the glory of God; Being justified freely by his grace through the redemption that is in Christ Jesus: (Rom. 3:20-24)

Perhaps it would be beneficial to hear the information presented from another Grace teacher we have considered before, William R. Newell. He offers a warning to those who ignore the free offer of salvation and summarizes the message of the Gospel of Grace as follows:

The failure or refusal to discern the Pauline Gospel as a separate and new revelation and not a "development from Judaism," accounts for two-thirds of the confusion in many people's minds today as regards just what the Gospel is. Paul's Gospel will suffer no admixture with works on the one hand or religious pretensions and performances on the other. It is as simple and clear as the sunlight from heaven.

The end of man is where God begins Romans 3, at what might be called the opening of the Pauline Revelation. Most unsaved people today believe in their hearts that the reason they are not saved is because of something they have not yet done, some step that remains for them to take before God will accept them. But this is absolutely untrue. When Christ

said, "It is finished," He meant that He had, then and there, paid the debt for the whole human race. "He gave Himself a ransom for all" (I Timothy 2:6).

Now Paul in his wonderful revelation declares that God hath reconciled the world to Himself; that God was in Christ (at the cross) reconciling the world unto Himself (II Corinthians 5:19). Men do not know this, but they conceive that something stands between them and God, before God will accept or forgive them.

If you tell a man that God is demanding no good works of him whatsoever, no religious observances or church ordinances, that God is not asking him to undertake any duties at all, but that God invites him to believe a glad message that his sins have already been dealt with at the cross, and that God expects him to believe this good news and be exceedingly happy about it - if you tell an unsaved man such a story as this, he is astonished and overwhelmed - yet this is the Gospel! (Newell 2011, 59-60)

Before we conclude this portion on the Pauline Epistles, it is important that the heart of the Gospel of Grace, which is recorded for us in summary form in First Corinthians, be examined in detail. Paul writes, "Moreover, brethren, I declare unto you the gospel which I preached unto you, which also ye have received, and wherein ye stand; *By which also ye are saved,* if ye keep in memory what I preached unto you, unless ye have believed in vain" (vv. 1-2). Continuing he tell them where he received his gospel, "For I delivered unto you first of all that which I also received . . ." (v.3a). He, having received the message directly from the Risen Lord, communicated the same to them. Concerning the unique message of Paul, Stam observes:

> Paul clearly states here that this is "the gospel which I preached unto you," and this was *not* the gospel which the twelve had been preaching. Otherwise, he would not habitually use such phrases as: "*my gospel*" (Three times: Rom. 2:16; 16:25; II Tim. 2:7,8); "*our gospel*" (Three times: II Cor. 4:3; I Thes. 1:5; II Thes. 2:14); "*the gospel which I preached unto you*" (I Cor. 15:1); "*the gospel which was preached of me*" (Gal. 1:11); "*that gospel which I preach among the Gentiles*" (Gal 2:2); and "that [gospel] which we preached unto you" (Gal. 1:8). (Stam 1992, 245-246)

Here it is: " . . . *Christ died for our sins* according to the scriptures; And that *he was buried, and that he rose again* the third day according to the scriptures" (vv. 3b-4). He then cites a list of witnesses that could testify to the authenticity of the resurrection of the Lord making it an historical fact. What makes this so unique from the Gospel of the Kingdom–the resurrection. Stam accentuates this point: "So, beloved, the secret of salvation, the key to heaven is contained in this simple statement of "five words" (1 Cor. 14:19): *"Christ died for our sins"* (l Cor. 15:3). And Paul, the chief of sinners, now saved by grace, was the herald and the living demonstration of this glorious truth."

The importance of this portion of Paul's gospel is confirmed in his words that follow: "Now if Christ be preached that he rose from the dead, how say some among you that there is no resurrection of the dead? But if there be no resurrection of the dead, then is Christ not risen: And if Christ be not risen, then is our preaching vain, and your faith is also vain" (vv. 12-14). Here the word "vain" means "producing no results or worthless." The importance of this for our purpose will be more evident as we look at the teaching from the Hebrew epistles which follow these Pauline epistles.

Finally, concerning this message, we must authenticate the messenger. In the second letter to the Corinthians, Paul opens his letter with, "Paul, an apostle of Jesus Christ by the will of God . . ." (2 Cor. 1:1) An apostle is a "messenger" and his installation into that position was by Jesus Christ Himself according to the will of God. Stam writes:

Again and again, in his epistles, Paul stresses his divine apostleship, and there is abundant proof that his claim is valid. He had never been formally trained for such a ministry as this; it was entirely God's doing. God chose him, called him, prepared and equipped him for it.

. . . This took place through a divine miracle when, on the road to Damascus, "breathing out threatenings and slaughter against the disciples of the Lord," he was suddenly converted to Christ as he *saw* the Jesus whom he had so bitterly persecuted . . . Right then and there the Lord not only forgave Paul of all his sins, but appointed him an apostle, to proclaim the most blessed message ever sent from God to man: *"the gospel of the grace of God."* (Stam 1992, 24)

The importance of not mixing anything to the formula of grace cannot be overemphasized. The Judaizers were constantly attacking Paul's doctrine trying, through subterfuge, to put the Grace believers back under the Law. He exhorts the Galatians,

"Stand fast therefore in the liberty wherewith Christ hath made us free, and be not entangled again with the yoke of bondage" (Gal. 5:1). Alva J. McClain was the founder and first president of Grace Theological Seminary and Grace College. He warns Christians not to mix grace with works:

> And so the problem becomes very simple: Either Christ will save you by grace through faith plus nothing, or He will not save you at all! As a matter of fact, even an omnipotent God can save sinners in only one way–that is, by grace. Because of what God is and because of what we are, there is no other way. Paradoxical as it may seem, this is one place where the addition of something finite actually results in a subtraction which is infinite. Such is the mathematics of grace. If the sinner adds anything, he loses everything. If he adds nothing, he wins everything. (McClain 2014, 53)

To coin a phrase familiar to my profession as an insurance agent for over thirty-five years, "Your policy is paid in full." Now, that is great news! Even more so, how wonderful it would be to hear the words, "Someone else paid the premium for you!" Such is the case concerning the offer for salvation. Although it is universal in its offer, it will only be effective for those who accept the offer while it is still available. The point in time when the unclaimed offer will be withdrawn is either the occurrence of your death or the Rapture, whichever comes first.

It is the Rapture that is the hope of the Church–the Body of Christ and how wonderful it will be to spend eternity with Our Lord and Savior Jesus Christ. Previously, we mentioned that there were two boundary markers. We discussed the first which was the conversion to Paul who was to be our pattern. Writing to Timothy, Paul states, "Howbeit for this cause, I obtained mercy, that in me first [as the prototype] Jesus Christ might shew forth all longsuffering, for a pattern [as an example] to them which should hereafter believe on him to life everlasting" (1 Tim. 1:16). Concerning our hope in Christ, Sadler writes, "Because Christ has conquered death and risen again. He has made our future resurrection certain. But, when will the hope of the resurrection be fulfilled? The answer to this question is, when Christ returns in the Rapture at the close of this dispensation."

Confirming the theory of the Rapture being the close of the Age of Grace, Sadler explains:

> ... We might look at it like this: Prior to Paul's revelation, the kingdom gospel required that a sinner "repent and be baptized" for the remission of his sins. With the raising up of the Apostle Paul, those who live in this age must believe Christ died for their sins, was buried, and rose again. We are forgiven by His shed blood. After our departure, the terms of salvation will revert back to the kingdom gospel. This means that only those who are redeemed under Paul's gospel are members of the Body of Christ and, therefore, partakers of the heavenly hope. We conclude, then, that the two landmarks of grace are *Paul's conversion* and the *Rapture of the Church*. (Sadler 1995, 125)

With the closing of the Age of Grace, which is a parenthetical interruption to Daniel's seventy weeks, the prophecy will be fulfilled with the appearing of the Antichrist. The seven remaining years are the trial of Israel called Jacob's Time of Trouble.

13

Hebrews

In our chiasmus, we declared that Hebrews, similar to the book of Acts, is a book of transition. We have seen the progression from the four Gospels being directed towards the children of Abraham with the offer of the Davidic kingdom and the presentation of their King. The book of Acts continued with the Jews being the focus at first; even at their rejection of the King. We are introduced to Paul at that point and the record of his conversion is recorded along with God's intention to send this chosen apostle to the Gentiles. Acts ends with these words. "Be it known therefore unto you [Jews], that the salvation of God is [now being] sent unto the Gentiles, and that they will hear it" (Acts 28:28). Paul continues to develop his doctrines as Acts progresses having received revelation directly from the ascended Lord Jesus Christ. Finally, Paul's epistles record the doctrine specific to his message–the Gospel of Grace–and the revelation of the Mystery which is "Christ in us the hope of glory." I consider Hebrews a book of transition not recorded within the text, but the first book transiting from the Age of Grace to the post-Rapture message to Jews. Let us examine why.

Concerning the book of Hebrews there is much contention. First, who wrote the book? Second, to whom was it written? Both Anderson and Stam each write considerably on the authorship of this book. Anderson writes, "The authorship of Hebrews has been a subject of controversy during all the centuries. Was it written by the Apostle whose name it bears in our English Bibles? . . . And the question at issue is purely one of evidence. It must be settled on the principles which govern the decisions of our Courts of Justice." Concerning the importance of the authorship, Stam writes, "The authorship of Hebrews is not only an interesting subject; it is of prime importance to a clear understanding of the Bible and especially of God's message and program for the present dispensation." Determining who the author is, has an effect on its dispensational interpretation, does it not? Yes. I intend to present a controversial supposition contrary to both the traditional Christendom as well as some of the leading theologians of the so-called *ultradispensational* position. Again, I believe that Hebrews was written for the needs of the God's elect after the Rapture.

Conservative theologians would ask the following questions: 1. Who wrote Hebrews? 2. To whom was it written? and 3. What was the intent of the author? I believe that the internal evidence which includes both writing styles and personal references support the Pauline authorship. However, I believe there was a good reason his authorship remains undisclosed. It was not written for the Church–the Body of Christ. Had he signed the letter, it would have been used by them to append their doctrine. If we could move forward with the assumption that Paul is the author, we can address the remaining two questions. We read in the opening line, "God, who at sundry times and in divers manners spake in time past unto the fathers by the prophets, Hath in these last days spoken unto us by his Son . . ." (Heb. 1:1-2).

The words "spake in time past unto the fathers by the prophets" would clearly point to the ancestors of the Jews; referring to the patriarchs. "Spoken unto us by his Son" would refer to the earthly ministry and preaching of the Messiah while He was among them. "Unto us" would mean that the writer would be included within that group which would exclude Paul, but may account for by Luke being the translator of Paul's original words from Greek to Hebrew.

The references, both at the beginning as well as throughout the letter, are found to be clearly directed to Jews who would understand such references as only they would.

The next question concerns the intent of the letter. As I mentioned the majority of conservatives believe that Hebrews was written to Christians who were of Jewish decent. However, the content of the letter is not a presentation of the Gospel of Grace to new believers; nor it is an exposition of teaching for the Church–the Body of Christ. It is a presentation of the Messiah as the High Priest of Israel of the order of Melchizedek. Melchizedek was a contemporary to Abraham called the King of Salem (King of Peace) to whom Abraham gave a tenth of his plunder. References are made to the Levitical Priesthood (v. 7:23), the Altar (13:10), the Offerings (10:10), the Tabernacle (8:20), the Holy of Holies (10:19, 20), and Baptisms "imposed on them until the time of reformation" (9:10).

The time of reformation is not about the Body of Christ, but the establishment of the Kingdom under their legitimate King. Here the Messiah will fulfill the prophecy of the New Covenant promised to Israel and Judah (*cf.* Jer. 31:31). Bear in mind that on the night He was betrayed, ". . . he took bread, and gave thanks, and brake it, and gave unto them, saying, "This is my body which is given for you: this do in remembrance of me." Likewise, also the cup after supper, saying, "This cup is the new testament [New Covenant] in my blood, which is shed for you" (Lk. 22:19-20). Here the Anointed One foreshadows His future position as Israel's High Priest, as we shall demonstrate.

Anderson writes, "For the divine scheme of prophecy relating to earth, as unfolded in the Old Testament, has definite reference to the covenant people; and their rejection of Christ seemed to thwart its fulfilment. But the sins of men cannot thwart the purposes of God . . ." Understanding that the Prophetic Plan is now in suspense and awaiting the completion of the current dispensation is very important here. He continues, "We have seen, however, that the grand scheme of Messianic prophecy relating to earth, though now in suspense, is in no way abrogated. It is therefore obvious to the intelligent student of Scripture that before it can be resumed the present 'economy' must be brought to a close."

We should consider if there is any portion of the New Testament the Jews may use which would provide them with additional revelation concerning their crucified Messiah. The answer is yes. I believe it concerns the three roles of their Messiah: Prophet, Priest, and King. Jesus came as the Prophet speaking to Israel on behalf of God. He is now acting as an intermediary on their behalf as their Priest providing continual intercession. When He returns at His Second Coming, He will be coming back as their victorious King!

In the book of Hebrews, it is my contention that the Messiah which they rejected is now acting on their behalf as their Priest, a better priest than that of the Levitical Priesthood. Stam disagrees, "Those who deny the present priesthood of Christ for the members of His Body, frequently argue: 'Why would we need a priest to bring us into God's presence? In Christ we are already there, seated in the heavenlies at God's right hand.'" Stam distinguishes from our *position* and our *condition*; our *standing* and our *state*. Speaking of our position he writes, "But is it not equally true that *experientially* we must *appropriate* this position again and again by faith?" I would ask, If we have the righteousness of Christ imputed to us as Grace Believers, then what is the need for continual appropriation? Paul writes, "But now the righteousness of God without the law is manifested . . . Even the righteousness of God which is by faith of Jesus Christ unto all and upon all them that believe: for there is no difference" (Rom. 3:21-22). Note that the last verse says by faith "of" Jesus Christ and not our faith "in" Jesus Christ. As much as it may steam some peoples' glasses, it is not about us; it is all about Him.

Donald Guthrie, in his book *New Testament Theology*, has two important comments on the book of Hebrews. This information might help us understand the author's intentions as he seeks to educate the Jews concerning the superiority of their New Covenant. Guthrie notes that Hebrews is concerned with the law as would be known by Israel; especially the ceremonial law:

> Generally, in this epistle *nomos* is used of the OT law. It is just possible that 7:16 might be understood in the sense of a legal ordinance, but even here a reference to the Mosaic requirements makes good sense. This epistle makes no distinction between the word used with or without the article. It is twice used in the plural, but only in quotations (8:10; 10:16). Sometimes the word is used in a restricted way of regulations relating to the cultus, but the writer does not distinguish between the moral and

ceremonial law, although he is mainly concerned with the latter. (Guthrie 1981, 697)

Israel's acceptance of the Covenant, to which they agreed in unison, bound them to all its contractual obligations. We read in Exodus:

> Now therefore, if ye will obey my voice indeed, and keep my covenant, then ye shall be a peculiar treasure unto me above all people: for all the earth is mine: And ye shall be unto me a kingdom of priests, and an holy nation. These are the words which thou shalt speak unto the children of Israel.
>
> And Moses came and called for the elders of the people, and laid before their faces all these words which the LORD commanded him. And all the people answered together, and said, All that the LORD hath spoken we will do. And Moses returned the words of the people unto the LORD. (Ex. 19:5-8)

The priestly system was instituted as part of the Mosaic Law which Moses presented to Israel as a new nation. Guthrie comments on this:

> The [priestly] system was designed to enable men to approach to God. The priests were 'appointed' (5:1), *i.e.* the whole institution was a provision of God. The epistle shows in many particulars the limitation of the system, particularly because death overtook all the appointed high priests and because their sacrifices had a limited effectiveness and could never take away sin, even their own (7:27). This epistle expounds the high-priestly theme, based as it was on the law, with the intention of showing its inadequacy. (Guthrie 1981, 698)

With this in view, it is my position that Hebrews was written by Paul to his beloved people. Happily, now as a Grace believer worshiping his God in spirit, he recounts the reasons why he considers himself worthy to be a considered a perfect Jew according to the Law. In Philippians, he writes:

For we are the circumcision, which worship God in the spirit, and rejoice in Christ Jesus, and have no confidence in the flesh. Though I might also have confidence in the flesh. If any other man thinketh that he hath whereof he might trust in the flesh, I more: Circumcised the eighth day, of the stock of Israel, of the tribe of Benjamin, an Hebrew of the Hebrews; as touching the law, a Pharisee; Concerning zeal, persecuting the church; touching the righteousness which is in the law, blameless. (Phil. 3:3-6)

The ultimate recipients of this book would be Paul's beloved Israel after the Rapture; so that they might read and understand what God has laid up for them in His divine plans. Paul expresses his anguish concerning his fellow countrymen even to the point of sacrificing himself, writing:

I say the truth in Christ, I lie not, my conscience also bearing me witness in the Holy Ghost, That I have great heaviness and continual sorrow in my heart. For I could wish that myself were accursed from Christ for my brethren, my kinsmen according to the flesh: Who are Israelites; to whom pertaineth the adoption, and the glory, and the covenants, and the giving of the law, and the service of God, and the promises; Whose are the fathers, and of whom as concerning the flesh Christ came, who is over all, God blessed forever. Amen. (Rom. 9:1-5)

Our time here as Grace Believers is drawing to a close. After the Rapture, Israel will remain. The elect of God and those who will attach themselves to Israel, the proselytes have seven years of testing ahead of them. May the words of our beloved Paul, written to his cherished people, give them comfort during their trial until the glorious coming of their King!

14

The Hebrew Epistles & Revelation

I considered Hebrews to be a transitional book moving us away from the distinct teachings of the Apostle Paul. At the Rapture, the Church–the Body of Christ will be removed from the earth. There are presently three divisions of humanity: Gentiles, Israel, and the Body of Christ. Now only two will remain. The seven-year period of time following the Rapture, known as Jacob's Time of Trouble, is a testing by God to find the "true" Israel. Those who are Gentiles will be saved, but that now depends on their relationship to Israel during this period of testing. Those Gentiles who support and care for Israel will be included in the Kingdom to come. However, the present dispensation, the Age of Grace, will close as God's Plan of Redemption moves on.

We cannot comment on the entire portion of the New Testament attributed to this final section of our proposed chiasmus due to the limitation of space. What we can examine is a good representation of the doctrine presented to the intended recipients. Although these epistles were written to Jews during the first century, they, more importantly, will apply to the Jews after the Rapture. We have selected Peter as a representative since he was the one chosen to be the Apostle to the Circumcision (*cf.* Gal. 2:8) and will be one of the twelve who will sit in judgment of Israel in the latter days. Sadler agrees with this position:

> We must always bear in mind that Peter's writings have a twofold purpose throughout. Under the guidance of the Holy Spirit, the aged apostle was addressing those then present and his countrymen in the future day of the Lord. We feel a greater emphasis of these periods is placed upon the latter of the two. Today, we turn to Paul's epistles for our doctrine and walk, but in the coming day of the Lord, the Tribulation saints will turn to the Hebrew Epistles for their marching orders.

While the fall of Israel occurred with the stoning of Stephen, the *casting away* of the favored nation was a gradual process which covered approximately a thirty year period. Thus, when Peter speaks about the "end of all things," "the fiery trial," and "judgment must begin at the house of God," he is preparing his hearers for the perilous times that lay ahead. Within five years of Peter putting the finishing touches on his epistles, Rome dispatched Titus to besiege the city of Jerusalem. This would be Israel's last stand nationally. (Sadler 2004, 139)

The siege of Titus in A.D. 70 was the event to which the Lord Jesus Christ referred in Matthew concerning primarily the temple but also Jerusalem in general. "And Jesus said unto them, See ye not all these things? verily I say unto you, There shall not be left here one stone upon another, that shall not be thrown down" (Matt. 24:2). At that point the current Diaspora (the scattering of Israel throughout the world amongst the Gentile nations) began which runs concurrent with the Times of the Gentiles. Remember back to our previous discussion concerning the 490 years prophesied by Daniel. These 490 years were interrupted by the cutting off of Israel's Anointed, our Savior Jesus Christ. At that point, a parenthetical period of time was created–the Mystery whereby both Jew and Gentile could be reconciled to God by His grace through faith without works. The Rapture closes the Age of Grace and the clock with its remaining seven years will resume its operation.

Paul Sadler was a wonderful Bible teacher and recently went home to be with his Savior. He summarizes so well the aspects of these last days that, in honor of him, I would like to include his comments in their entirety:

> As the curtain of the present dispensation is drawn to a close at the Rapture, it will immediately be followed by the time of *Jacob's Trouble*. Israel will again be center stage as the final drama of the Prophetic Program unfolds. In the coming day of the Lord, those of the future Jewish dispersion who read Peter's words will understand that they too are about to face a similar fate as their forefathers. This time, however, it is not Rome,

but the Anti-Christ who will oppress them.

As the Anti-Christ rises to power through flatteries, he will establish a covenant with the chosen nation, which essentially allows her to *reestablish* the sacrificial system in Jerusalem at the beginning of the Tribulation. In the middle of the Tribulation he breaks the covenant with Israel. He will then enter the temple, which defiles it in the sight of God. This is the abomination of desolation!

The Lord warned those who will live in that day, "When ye therefore shall see the abomination of desolation, spoken of by Daniel the prophet, stand in the holy place, (whoso readeth, let him understand:)" (Matt. 24:15). Notice, when they "see," that is, see the Anti-Christ enter the temple to declare himself to be God. When they behold this event, they are to immediately flee Jerusalem, for the armies of the Gentiles will soon occupy the city (Rev. 11:1,2). This will be the man of sin's death machine that will pursue Israel with the swiftness of a leopard attacking its prey. Nearly one-half of the world's population will have perished by the middle of the Tribulation, between the wrath of God being poured out on this Christ-rejecting world and the genocide caused by the Anti-Christ. But this is only the beginning of sorrows, for the worst is yet to come in the latter part of the Tribulation, known as the Great Tribulation. The Apostle John calls this period the "hour of trial."

In that day, the inhabitants of the earth will be required to worship the image of the Beast, a lifelike *idol* of the Anti-Christ. They will have little choice in the matter, it's either worship him or be executed on the spot! Moreover, the man of sin will cause both small and great to receive the Mark of the Beast-666.

The number six in the Scriptures is

the number of man. God created man on the sixth day, his average height is six feet, his workweek is six days, and he is normally buried six feet under. This is a solemn reminder that the Anti-Christ is not God, but merely a man, albeit a very powerful man. Those who refuse to receive the number of his name will be unable to buy or sell. This will place the Israelites in a quandary in that day, simply because those who receive this mark will be eternally damned (Rev. 13:11-18 cf. 14:9-12).

We cannot begin to fathom the intensity of the fiery trials that the future Tribulation saints will be called upon to endure. It does, however, give you a greater appreciation that we are living in the age of grace. Thankfully, we've been delivered from the wrath to come. (Sadler 2004, 141-143)

The above is a summary of the remaining seven years of prophecy according to the Old Testament as well as the words spoken by the Lord Jesus

Christ while here on earth. Our contention has been that these Hebrew epistles and the book of Revelation will be available to Israel during her testing. Much like the four Gospels which present to Israel her King, these final letters are for Israel and her proselytes' encouragement and consolation during the coming Tribulation. These present the Messiah as their Prophet, their Priest, and, ultimately, their King. These books complete the arrangement of the New Testament as a chiasmus.

15

Conclusion

It was almost twenty years ago that I was attending a weekly Bible study in the home of Pastor Henry Harding. Rocky, as his friends called him, presented those in attendance with a small booklet entitled *Rightly Dividing the Word of Truth* written by the late Dr. C. I. Scofield. That book encouraged me to believe the Bible could make sense. It was here that I chose as my personal charge to "Study to shew thyself approved unto God, a workman that needeth not to be ashamed, rightly dividing the word of truth" (2 Tim. 2:15). In the introduction of this booklet, he writes:

> The Word of Truth, then, has right divisions, and it must be evident that, as one cannot be "a workman that needeth not to be ashamed" without observing them, so any

study of that Word which ignores those divisions must be in large measure profitless and confusing. Many Christians freely confess that they find the study of the Bible weary work. More find it so, who are ashamed to make the confession.

The purpose of this pamphlet is to indicate the more important divisions of the Word of Truth. That this could not be fully done short of a complete analysis of the Bible is, of course, evident; but it is believed that enough is given to enable the diligent student to perceive the greater outlines of truth, and something of the ordered beauty and symmetry of that Word of God which, to the natural mind, seems a mere confusion of inharmonious and conflicting ideas.

The student is earnestly exhorted not to receive a single doctrine upon the authority of this book, but, like the noble Bereans (Acts 17: 11), to search the SCRIPTURES daily whether these things are so. No appeal is made to human authority. (Scofield n.d., 3)

Years later, when I traveled to Florida to meet with Dr. Nathan Killian about admission to Evangelical Theological Seminary, I stayed with friends in Orlando. While sitting at the kitchen table with J. R. Lawrence, his wife Pam, and son James, we had a most incredible theological discussion. As a dispensationalist, he encouraged me to continue examining Scriptures from a dispensational perspective; reminding me that it was only a tool. He also recommended my first theology book, Ryrie's *Dispensationalism Today*. From that point on, I was committed to understanding the Bible based upon answering the questions "Who wrote it?", "To whom was it written?", and "What was the context and message the author was conveying?" This dissertation was intended to present my findings to-date.

In the opening chapters I asked that the reader keep an open mind and, if you have made it to this point, you no doubt have done so. Clyde Pilkington, Jr. is Bible teacher and evangelist. He offers these words of encouragement, "What a life-long task every workman of the Scriptures has. It involves never allowing ourself to be locked into *any* man-made creed or systematic theology; while cultivating an ever-adjusting heart and mind to what has been learned afresh from the Scriptures. It requires a mental and spiritual of openness.

He suggests that we continue to be open to biblical preaching, listen willingly and then compare it to what is taught in the Scriptures. Pilkington goes on to explain that there is a division within Scripture and understanding that is critical to interpretation:

> The Word of God itself provides us with the key to its own proper understanding through *"rightly dividing the Word of Truth."* God's ecclesia, the Body of Christ, is not the only people in the programs and purposes of God. People in other ages need Scripture to instruct them in the specifics of God's dealings with them just as we do. Remember that all the Scripture is *for* us – but it is not all *to* us, nor is it all *about* us. If we fail to recognize this important fact, we will never be able to properly understand just what God is doing today, nor will we know just what He would have us do. (Pilkin-

ton 2009, 68)

There are three objections I receive when explaining this to someone new to the idea of "rightly dividing." The first is that it creates unique groups. That idea is highly offensive to some because of its discriminatory nature. For those who wish to interpret Scripture based upon their own individual fancy, there is nothing I can say. Another accused me of being a Gnostic because he felt that it is exclusive knowledge only to initiates. This tool is available to anyone who will use it. The most popular objection has to do with our democratic thinking where our choice is determined by those with whom we associate and is accredited by the size of the congregation. One of the most well-known evangelicals at the time is Joel Osteen. His webpage states:

> On July 16, 2005, after completing $95 million dollars in renovations, Joel moved Lakewood Church into its new 16,000-seat home - the former Compaq Center. It is the largest regularly-used worship center in the United States. Each week Joel delivers God's message of hope and encouragement to more than 38,000 attendees. According to Nielsen Media

Research, Joel is the most watched inspirational figure in America.

It would appear that this evangelist is a model by which other Christians should emulate. His website goes on to explain his success:

> Joel's extraordinary success can be found in his core message: That our God is a good God who desires to bless those who are obedient and faithful to Him through Jesus Christ. It is Joel's deepest desire that his own life be an example of that principle and that everyone who hears this message of hope and encouragement would choose to accept God's goodness and mercy and to become all that God wants them to be. (www.joelosteen.com)

The purpose for my including comments about Joel Osteen is to disparage neither him personally nor his ministry. He is an example of what we just stated above. His message, like that of Rick Warren, is one of success with the goal of leading a happy and content life. This is certainly not what the Lord Jesus Christ taught in His earthly ministry, nor did Paul!

Compare this to what Paul told Timothy, "Yea, and all that will live godly in Christ Jesus shall suffer persecution" (2 Tim. 3:12). This is just an example of how we need to listen to what is being taught and then compare it to our sole guide and authority for our life as believers–the Holy Scriptures!

As those who are abiding in this current dispensation called the Age of Grace, we must be cognizant of two concerns: our salvation and the salvation of others. Most are satisfied with attending a church weekly. To those I suggest that the majority of churches today in Christendom will be operating as usual, with most of the members in attendance, the Sunday after the Rapture. Then, it will be too late. To survive, then, they must align themselves with Israel as the only remaining source of salvation. Pilkington, in his incredible book called *The Church in Ruins*, makes some excellent points worth considering:

> Paul's instruction to Timothy is of a very personal and individual nature throughout this epistle. The believers in Asia were now outside of the teachings and practices of Paul. They had turned away from him. They were now embracing the religious system; a "Christian" religious sys-

tem that is "Christendom." Without Paul's message, that is all one has - RELIGION.

Timothy therefore now finds himself on the *outside* of the activities of the believers. Interestingly enough, Paul never instructs Timothy anywhere in this epistle to "go in" among them and see if he could "turn the tide." Instead of ministering to "a congregation," "a church," "an assembly," or "his parishioners," Paul tells Timothy to *"find faithful men."* Timothy was to seek out men, *"faithful men"* to whom he could commit Paul's message.

Paul had no thought of Asia ever being "revived." Instead, because of the apostasy, his instruction to Timothy concerning the ministry of the Word had now become extremely narrow, intensely individual – *"faithful men!"* (Pilkington 2009, 49)

How is the church doing with Paul's instructions given to Timothy? The church, Christendom as we know it, is in ruins. Paul was as right then as he is now, "Preach the word; be instant in season, out of season; reprove, rebuke, exhort with all long suffering and doctrine. For the time will come when they will not endure sound doctrine; but after their own lusts shall they heap to themselves teachers, having itching ears" (2 Tim. 4:2-3).

A dispensational method of interpretation yields clarity of message to anyone diligent enough to search for it. I believe with my whole being that Christ is God Himself, and He died on Calvary to pay for all my sins – past, present, and future. Then, He arose from the grave a Victor because His sacrifice was accepted by Almighty God. We have been reconciled to God! We must continue to rely solely on His work as being sufficient; any actions or works which are added as a requirement for salvation diminishes its sufficiency and turns it to naught. Now that you have finished reading this paper, be like the noble Bereans, who "searched the scriptures daily, [to see] whether those things were so" (Acts 17:11).

Bibliography

Anderson, Sir Robert. *The Silence of God.* Mansfield Centre, Conn.: Martino Publishing, 2011.

_____. *Types In Hebrews.* Grand Rapids, Mich.: Kregel Publications, 1978.

_____. *The Coming Prince.* Updated ed. Lawton, Okla.: Trumpet Press, 2014.

Chafer, Lewis Sperry. *Systematic Theology.* 4 vols. Grand Rapids: Kregel Publications, 1976.

Cho, David Yonggi. *The Apocalyptic Prophecy – Reconciling Today's Global Events With End-Time Prophecy.* Lake Mary, Fla.: Creation House, 1998.

Conybeare, W. J., and J. S. Howson. *The Life and Epistles of St. Paul.* Grand Rapids, Mich.: Wm. B. Eerdmans Publishing Company, 1954.

Enns, Paul. *The Moody Handbook of Theology*. Revised and expanded ed. Chicago: Moody Publishers, 2008.

Geisler, Norman L. *Christian Apologetics*. 2nd printing. Peabody, Mass.: Prince Press div. of Hendrickson Publishers, 2003.

Guthrie, Donald. *New Testament Theology*. Downers Grove, Ill.: InterVarsity Press, 1981.

Hunt, Dave. *What Love is This?–Calvinism's Misrepresentation of God*. 3rd ed. Bend, Ore.: The Berean Call, 2006.

Hodge, Charles. *Systematic Theology*. Abridged ed. Edited by Edward N. Gross. Phillipsburg, NJ: Presbyterian and Reformed Publishing Co., 1997.

Larkin, Clarence. *Dispensational Truth or God's Plan and Purpose in the Ages*. Mansfield Centre, Conn.: Martino Publishing, 2011.

Lightner, Robert P. *Sin, the Savior, and Salvation–The Theology of Everlasting Life*. Grand Rapids: Kregel Publications, 1991.

McClain, Alva J. *Law and Grace–A Study of New Testament Concepts as They Relate to the Christian Life*. 9th printing. Winona Lake, Ind.: BMH Books, 2014.

_____. *Paul vs. Peter*. 2nd ed. Windber, Penn.: Bible Student's Press, 2009.

Pilkington, Jr., Clyde L. *The Church In Ruins*. Windber, Penn.: Bible Student's Press, 2009.

Pentecost, J. Dwight. *Things to Come–A Study in Biblical Eschatology*. 1st printing. Grand Rapids, Mich.: Zondervan, 1964.

Perschbacher, Wesley J. ed. *The New Analytical Greek Lexicon*. 9th printing. Peabody, Mass.: Hendrickson Publishers, 2006.

Ryrie, Charles C. *Basic Theology–A Popular Systematic Guide to Understanding Biblical Truth*. Chicago: Moody Press, 1999.

_____. *Dispensationalism*. Rev. and expanded. Chicago: Moody Publishers, 2007.

Scofield, C. I. *Rightly Dividing the Word of Truth*. Fincastle, Vir.: Scripture Truth Book Co., n.d.

Showers, Renald E. *There Really Is A Difference–A Comparison of Covenant and Dispensational Theology*.

13th ed. Bellmawr, N.J.: The Friends of Israel Gospel Ministry, 2013.

Sadler, Paul M. *The Triumph Of His Grace–Preparing Ourselves for the Rapture.* 2nd printing. Germantown, Wisc.: Berean Bible Society, 1995.

_____. *Exploring The Unsearchable Riches of Christ–The Key That Unlocks The Sacred Secret.* 5th printing. Germantown, Wisc.: Berean Bible Society, 2011.

Spencer, Duane Edward. *TULIP–The Five Points of Calvinism in the Light of Scripture.* Grand Rapids: Baker Books, 1979

Stam, Cornelius R. *Acts–Dispensationally Considered.* 2 vols. 6th printing. Germantown, Wisc.: Berean Bible Society, 2011.

_____. *Colossians–The Preeminence of Christ.* 1st printing. Germantown, Wisc.: Berean Bible Society, 2002.

_____. *Commentary on the First Epistle of Paul to the Corinthians.* 2nd printing. Germantown, Wisc.: Berean Bible Society, 2005.

_____. *Commentary on the Second Epistle of Paul to*

the Corinthians. 2nd printing. Germantown, Wisc.: Berean Bible Society, 1992.

_____. *Galatians–Law vs. Grace.* 2nd printing. Germantown, Wisc.: Berean Bible Society, 2006.

_____. *Commentary on the Pastoral Epistles of Paul the Apostle.* 2nd printing. Germantown, Wisc.: Berean Bible Society, 1983.

_____. *The Epistle to the Hebrews–Who Wrote It and Why?* Stevens Point, Wisc.: Worzalla Publishing Co., 1991.

_____. *Things That Differ–The Fundamentals of Dispensationalism.* 15th printing. Germantown, Wisc.: Berean Bible Society, 2008.

Tenney, Merrill C. *New Testament Survey.* Revised ed. Grand Rapids, Mich.: Wm. B. Eerdmans Publishing Company, 1985.

Vine, W.E. *Vine's Expository Dictionary of Old & New Testament Words.* Nashville: Thomas Nelson, 1997.

Zuck, Roy B. *Basic Bible Interpretation–A Practical Guide to Discovering Biblical Truth.* Colorado Springs, Colo.: David C. Cook, 1991.

Other GraceWord Publications

Complete Surveys Of The Bible:

Letters To Theophilus
The Glorious Destiny Of Israel
The Hidden Gospel: Once Hidden But Now Reveal.

Expositional Commentaries Of The Bible:

1st Corinthians: Dispensationally Considered
1st & 2nd Thessalonians: Disp. Considered
1st & 2nd Timothy & Titus: Disp. Considered
2nd Corinthians: Dispensationally Considered
Acts: Dispensationally Considered
Colossians & Philemon: Disp. Considered
Ephesians: Dispensationally Considered
Galatians: Dispensationally Considered
Hebrews: Dispensationally Considered
Philippians: Dispensationally Considered
Revelation: Dispensationally Considered
Romans: Dispensationally Considered

The Gospel of John: Dispensationally Considered
The Gospel of Luke: Dispensationally Considered
The Gospel of Mark: Dispensationally Considered
The Gospel of Matthew: Disp. Considered
The Seven Hebrew Epistles: Disp. Considered

Other Books

How Am I Wired?
Two Distinct Gospel Messages Of The N.T.

About The Author

The author has over thirty-five years of experience as an insurance agent managing a multi-state independent agency selling both property and casualty as well as life insurance. Now retired, he continues to devote much of his time to understanding the Bible from the viewpoint of primacy for both Jewish and Christian doctrine.

He obtained his Bachelor of Theology, Master of Biblical Studies, and Ph.D. in Biblical Studies from Evangelical Theological Seminary where he holds a position of adjunct professor. He also holds a Ph.D. in Christian Counseling from Cornerstone University.

He wrote his dissertation on viewing the same Bible from the three systems of theology, those predominantly held by evangelical churches today. Each system yields a different interpretation. He examined each of them. His dissertation was originally published under the name Understanding Scripture:

Using the Literary Structure of the New Testament. Now, the book is published under a new name Two Distinct Gospel Messages Of The New Testament: Using The Literary Structure Of The New Testament.

Dr. Greene endeavors to follow Paul's example. It was Paul who said he was the least of all saints much like the author and many other Christians. It is never about us, but about Him who is able to do exceedingly abundantly above all that we ask or think. It is His Spirit Who works through us.

Paul said that much grace was given to him that he should preach among the Gentiles the unsearchable riches of Christ. He goes on to say that he wished to make all men see what is the fellowship of the mystery, which from the beginning of the world had been hid in God.

It is the author's desire that you may see what is the fellowship of the mystery so that you too may be *in Christ* forever.

www.ingramcontent.com/pod-product-compliance
Lightning Source LLC
Chambersburg PA
CBHW071721120626
46550CB00001B/335